Eye in the Last Storm

Eye in the Last Storm

A Reporter's Journal of One Year in Southeast Asia

James Willwerth

Grossman Publishers   New York   1972

Acknowledgments

Eye in the Last Storm is a pastiche of impressions laid down in journal form which began, more or less, as a series of notes to myself. Its completion owes much to friends and colleagues who offered encouragement along the way. Early critics of the manuscript include Susan Shearer, Linley Stafford, Ron Ridenhour, Susan Rosen, Marsh Clark, and Rebecca White. Professionally, Frank McCulloch, Marsh Clark, Jon Larsen, Murray J. Gart and Henry A. Grunwald, my various bosses at *Time*, influenced and aided this effort in a variety of ways. I am particularly grateful to McCulloch, a father figure to scores of present and former *Time* journalists, for helping me get to Viet Nam in the first place. And I owe a debt to Henry Aronson, formerly of the Lawyers Military Defense Committee in Saigon, for his advice on dealing with the publishing world. Finally, my thanks to Ellyn Polshek, my editor, whose literary abilities are surpassed only by her talents as a psychoanalyst.

To my mother, Margaret V. Willwerth, also a reporter.

And to the memory of those who died
covering the Indochina wars.

Contents

Foreword   *xi*

1

Arriving   *3*
First Briefing   *7*
Politics   *9*
The GI   *12*
Darkness   *15*
Tina   *16*

2

Never-Never Land   *20*
Messages from Washington   *22*
Messages from Home   *24*
Scenes   *25*
Firefight   *29*
Thank You, Mr. President   *33*
Exodus   *35*

3

First Aid, American Style   *40*
Death and Diplomacy   *42*
A Friend   *44*
Death in Little Boxes   *46*
Coming Out   *49*
American Girl   *52*

4

The Pilot *54*

The Upside-Down Man *56*

Analysis of Sorts *59*

Airport Scene *62*

5

Say, Can You See? *66*

A Short One at O'Reilly's *68*

On the River *71*

One Future *73*

The Sporting Life *75*

Trinh Phu *78*

Bombs Away *83*

More Bombs *87*

6

Raindrops *90*

The Street Kid *95*

Boredom and (a Little) Madness *97*

Folly at Five O'Clock *99*

A Spy Story *101*

On Being a Westerner *104*

Cu Chi *106*

Merry Christmas *112*

Chi Ba *114*

7

Laos Coming   *118*

Show Business   *119*

Quang Tri   *121*

The Last Invasion   *123*

Invasion Day   *129*

All the News   *133*

My Friend, the Hired Killer   *134*

Dear Somebody   *137*

Larry Burrows   *139*

Press Problems   *141*

Winning the War   *145*

8

Coming Down   *149*

Waiting to Go Home . . .   *152*

Street Scene   *154*

Another Bar Girl   *155*

On American Values   *157*

Antihero   *159*

Good-bye   *162*

A Little Love   *165*

Cambodia: The Last Time   *168*

The Great Brass Caper   *170*

Going Home   *177*

Foreword

This is a personal story. It avoids politics and history whenever possible. It barely mentions military strategy, and offers only scattered notes on government issues. If prominent individuals, American or Vietnamese, are mentioned, it is as a convenience. As a reporter I write about public people and political abstractions regularly, and I believe there is value in this. Viet Nam, I discovered during my time there, asks more of you, for I found that the country forced itself behind my professional exterior. Soon I became concerned with experiences: the war's dynamics as they affected me. And the people I could see or talk to as I traveled around Indochina.

Altogether more than a million human beings have died since the people of Southeast Asia first began to tire of colonialism. For my country, the cost of Viet Nam has been nearly fifty thousand lives, at least $120 billion, untold agony. And Indochina has touched all of us, usually tragically. Thus, after living at home with this war for nearly a decade, first as a student, then a journalist, I wanted to know Viet Nam personally rather than simply feel its imprint in New York City or Berkeley. And so I volunteered to go to Southeast Asia for *Time* magazine.

Many books have been written about the Viet Nam war, and this is probably the laziest to date. It attempts no organization other than a chronological one—diary notes, kept and recorded as things happened that I wanted to write about. And, each entry is an event more or less independent of the rest, though they all have an obvious connection: a ball of string unraveled, which was my experience in Southeast Asia. (I say Southeast Asia, incidentally, because the Viet Nam war in reality is a regional conflict, and during my time there it was publicly pushed across both the Cambodian and Laotian borders.)

I recall an article in *Time* magazine after Green Berets attempted in 1970 to rescue American prisoners of war in Son Tay, North Viet Nam, beginning: "Once again, like a recurring jungle fever, Viet Nam has forced itself to the front of the nation's consciousness." That seems an apt—if unfortunate—summary. For while the war *is* something you want to forget, it refuses to leave us. As it happened, my time in Asia encompassed the last major ground combat thrusts—Cambodia and Laos—by American soldiers in this war. Yet even as this book went to press, Viet Nam was convulsed by an invasion from the North, and Americans, in turn, were deeply divided over this country's proper role in the emergency.

I should add, I suppose, that during my year in Viet Nam and Cambodia, I found nothing to alter my college-bred skepticism about the war—though I admit to considerable sympathies for the predicament of some South Vietnamese.

But enough of this. My objective is not to talk about politics or the "meaning" of Viet Nam. Too much has been written, and I think the question is best left to the Vietnamese. I prefer to tell a story which might interest readers unable to follow the intricacies of politics and diplomacy closely: how Southeast Asia looked to the mind's eye.

JKW, New York,
Spring, 1972

1

New York, Spring 1970

"A reporter?"

I nodded. The elderly clerk in Rockefeller Center, face lined like onion-skin, took the money and began to make notes on my passport application. After a moment he looked across the counter at me, squinting, then suddenly leaned forward and said in a flinty voice:

"I hope you'll be more objective . . ." He stiffened and continued loudly. ". . . than some of those reporters over there."

I was caught off balance, and I bristled. But then, as he handed me a receipt, I only laughed. "Sure, I'll do my best . . ." I looked straight into his eyes. ". . . okay?"

I was bluffing, smiling, but deeply angry: no one likes to be told how to do his job. And I was embarrassed, for he'd struck a nerve. I do worry about objectivity and honest reporting, and I know that Viet Nam after ten years has brought us to a national anger that all too often shatters even polite conversation. Families are split. A President resigns. Young men leave the country. A passport clerk lashes out, and I react in heat and confusion.

Back at the office a senior editor shrugged when I said I was going. "It's still a story." He paused: ". . . I guess," and he wished me luck without enthusiasm. Few friends approved of the trip—reckless adventuring and too late. The war seemed over. GIs were coming home, and most Americans were dovish or at least impatient it couldn't be won John Wayne style.

But something pulled me. Perhaps the simple need to follow lives and ideas crossing the Pacific this decade, a story no journalist could avoid. Then, too, an urge to test troubled thoughts, myths fragmenting, of America—

1

formed during classes at Berkeley and tested in New York covering war protests—by going to the source of them.

And perhaps—I wanted to hide this, but it was more urgent than I admitted—the chance to escape a very personal pain, a woman gone and love corroded: the wound seething in part from lost innocence. I wanted to run in any direction offering light. Even fire.

The old clerk, then, wanted stories to make Viet Nam seem right. But I wanted it to be real, in all its horror, a place where I could be truly pulled apart and reassembled. So I took that passport and closed my apartment and put my furniture in storage. A typewriter and an airline ticket and it was time to go.

Arriving

I am thinking of holes in the ground, clusters of punctures in the country's skin, as the plane descends. They stretch in all directions from Saigon, long lines of pinprick patterns enlarged to huge craters as we approach earth. Below are people who endure the bombs like seasonal monsoons, and I wonder what is left of their lives. How much rain before they are swept away?

The plane's wheels hit the hot runway with a heavy squeak, and we taxi through checkerboard patterns of sandbag barriers and concrete walls that protect military planes, private aircraft, and commercial jets from mortars. Sunshine and steam whoosh in as the plane opens like a vacuum can, and through this I walk woodenly toward a flat building, under an awning, through a corridor. My new bureau chief, Marsh Clark, is waiting in the corridor, and I must be an odd picture to him. A thin, nervous man-boy in a gray business suit carrying a guitar I don't play yet.

I am sweating already and reach to loosen the tie tightened minutes ago to impress him. He makes it easy, saying take off the jacket, too. I am straining, caught in the heat and intensity of the moment, rendered waxen, stiff yet vulnerable as my body moves through appointed tasks—muted dealings about passports and luggage and the sharp slamming of inky stamps under clicking ceiling fans—and out.

The road into Saigon is a river of oily smoke jammed with thin bronze figures rushing furiously forward. Thousands of Asian faces over broomstick bodies on Hondas and motorbikes flashing in the sun, handle to handle, pushing and shoving to spawn and die. They fill both lanes, cut in front of each other, swerve out of side streets, fumes merging into mist. I am half talking to Clark, who drives, and watching all this. The clamor of life and machinery in motion is staggering.

We pass whole blocks of barbed wire, men everywhere with guns, military trucks. My mind races. There is energy here like a bomb bursting or a beehive overturned. Faces emerge from endless shanties of tin and wood. The colors are kaleidoscopic. It is a city of darkness and light, the graceful capital of a rice and fishing culture tilting toward chaos. Huge villas look over high walls to refugee camps. The tall trees lining the avenues die from air pollution. Saigon has ten times the people its planners envisioned, and more are coming—more shacks and shanty towns, beggars and barbed wire.

The streets merge in midtown. From the car I stare up at the museum-sized Continental Palace Hotel bathed in heat waves. The magazine has an office on the second floor filled with typewriters, telex copy and cluttered in spirit by the barnacles of old stories. Across the street, the National Assembly Building, once an opera house, fills the block like a beached white whale. Daily press briefings are a diagonal walk across Tu Do Street in the sweaty National Press Building, a warren of ink-stained cubicles in a decaying French colonial office building. Before the American war, traffic-glutted Tu Do was an elegant shopping arcade. Now the shops compete with bars, and Vietnamese women buying silk and ivory are outnumbered by girls who sell themselves.

The hotel reeks of old drama, images of movie classics flashing before the lens of my eye like nickelodeon frames. Actors from past and present wars sit on the veranda holding tall drinks brought by white-suited waiters. They lounge about the lobby, blankly watching passersby, talking to one another with sidelong glances. Novelist Graham Greene painted this picture in *The Quiet Amer-*

ican, and eighteen years later his characters and the hotel look the same: spies and journalists, diplomats and military men, call girls and war profiteers, all framed by long dark hallways with mute roomboys sliding about, potted plants, ceiling fans.

Fantasy becomes reality. My mind absorbs both as we walk in. On a rainy night a few months from now, the wind blowing darkness before it, a stranger in a safari suit will approach me in the lobby, point his umbrella like a gun, and ask half jokingly about Godot. His eyes are opaque, seeking a chance answer to a common riddle —from yet another stranger—to pull him out of some psychic bog. He is drowning, waving that umbrella desperately. I can't help and I am unnerved by the reflection in his face. I turn away into the night.

Meet *Time*'s Vietnamese staff, all smiles and handshakes. Nguyen Thuy Dang (Dang), the deceptively easygoing office manager who is an officer in the army's psy-war department. Madame Nga Tran Thi (Madame Nga), portly and always smiling, who keeps the books and can get you a good rate on the black market. Le Minh, the half-Chinese photographer and fixer who makes enough money on the side to send his children to school in America. Co, a wispy girl who runs errands and works the telex. Pham Xuan An (An), an aging reporter-guru with genuine warmth and excellent sources. An Nguyen Ngoc, the driver, a dull, beefy fellow who grins whenever you approach but is said to work for the secret police. Luu Nguyen Duc (Luu) and Long Luong Xich (Long), telex operators who work at night to supplement their military salaries.

The word is already out that I am young—Le Minh checked my passport at the airport—and they disapprove a little. Clark, who is tall and thin with heavy eyes, says to relax and look around for a few days. He looks tired, as though he works and lives harder than he should. But he is warm and easygoing, and we will have a long

First Briefing

Each Friday at the barnlike MACV (Military Assistance Command, Viet Nam) headquarters—an endless collection of intersecting hallways dubbed Pentagon East by the press—they have a briefing for new correspondents. It is a dull and sleep-inducing exercise conducted in a hot, tiny room. The briefers are men who know you don't believe them: overstarched career military officers and a chubby bureaucrat from the Pacification program. My sleepy mind quickly turns him into a traveling encyclopedia salesman. The military men merge into a row of polished gray tombstones.

The briefing soon becomes a thinly disguised psy-war exercise—aimed at the audience. Both the army and navy briefers point out that the "enemy" uses the foreign press to get its propaganda out. They say this almost apologetically, as if it pains them to give us the bad news. The navy guy, a rotund, fatherly fellow, smiles a lot and tells us his experiences in Viet Nam aren't reflected in the press reports he sees in the United States. He's been a reporter in Washington for nine years, he says, so he knows all about journalism. A real tiger. He probably edited a navy alumni newsletter.

At least one hour has passed and I'm getting sleepy.

The Air Force briefer, an enthusiastic captain, says almost in sorrow: "It's hard to believe that it has been two years since we stopped bombing the North." He misses the old days. Another hour. We are shown pictures of every plane the United States has in Viet Nam.

It is the army man who makes the day. He points to an area just over the Cambodian border, where headquarters for the Communist war effort is assumed to be, lamenting it can't be bombed. One bright note: it was run by a

7

four-star general who had pull with Hanoi policymakers. Then one day Hanoi radio said the general had died of a heart attack.

"But *our* intelligence indicates," grins this jug-eared trooper from the Corn Belt, "that he was killed during a B-52 bombing raid."

And the major stands there a few seconds more and smiles at us, like it's the best news he's heard since the Saigon PX acquired chewing tobacco. He knows that a B-52 raid is the best approximation of pure hell yet invented: tons of fire raining from huge planes flying so high that men neither see nor hear them coming. It is said that some people on the ground are beaten to death in their bunkers by blast concussions.

Another hour. We conclude with a Pacification talk by the jolly bureaucrat. He says his people are making "progress" and the "prognosis" is continued progress. My head hurts and I am bored, though I admit the briefings were useful. Viet Nam appears to be a country where you have to understand perfectly how complicated things are in order to disagree intelligently with dozens of other interpretations of the same facts. About four hours after I walked into that uncomfortable room, I was on my way.

Politics

I'm having lunch today with Pham Xuan An, our Vietnamese reporter. He doesn't *write* for us, since that would quickly get him into trouble with the government. He talks to Vietnamese sources and passes on the intelligence.

An is thin and slightly bent, a scholarly man whose combination of mind and body make me think of intricate lines meeting at sharp angles. He is a complex man, thoughtful and quiet, yet compelling when he talks about his country.

He seems surprised when I suggest a Vietnamese restaurant. We have fish soup, pork cooked in coconut milk, spiced pork, pickle rind and rice. While we eat, a kid enters the restaurant and sings loudly. His little sister walks around and holds out a cup.

Over lunch, Viet Nam sounds enormously Byzantine: a mosaic of rice fields planted and tilled by many hands, some unseen. The country is being destroyed by war, yet it has become dependent on it. Vietnamese politics are so conspiratorial and factionalized that only the war effort keeps the government together. American money also props it up. If there were a ceasefire, the government would probably come apart. Soldiers would desert and return to their families. Politicians would desert President Nguyen Van Thieu in order to seek power for themselves.

As American money coming into the country slowed down, most of Viet Nam's economic apparatus would disintegrate. The country has little or no industry and imports at least twenty-five times as many consumer goods as it exports. The economy is based almost completely on American war and Pacification programs. When these go, so do the jobs they've created. Then the

Hondas will run out of gas. Inflation will set in, social discontent will rise.

Meanwhile, An goes on (while I struggle to absorb this) the government and the army, both led by a French-educated upper class, continue to indulge in political intrigue and corruption. They know the Americans will leave eventually, so they consolidate their respective positions and save money for the day they may have to flee or buy themselves out of a tight situation.

President Thieu is highly unpopular and a ruthless politician. He becomes more isolated each day, and though he seems to have a stable government, plus an improving military and pacification situation, it is due primarily to solid American backing, and images created by public relations and the manipulation of statistics. No one will challenge him seriously, says An, while the Americans support him—though opponents would surface immediately if they didn't. Ngo Dinh Diem fell only when the Americans withdrew their support, so for now Thieu is solidly entrenched. This doesn't mean that South Viet Nam grows healthier.

"It is impossible to be popular in Viet Nam because there are so many factions," smiles An, lighting a Lucky Strike with bony hands and smiling as a teacher might. "When you say Thieu is strong, you have to ask: relative to what?"

The North Vietnamese, he continues, have no need for an immediate military victory. Nor do they have the manpower for one. They need only to have a strong infrastructure of political cadres in the South while keeping military pressure on Thieu until the Americans leave. Eventually, the North Vietnamese feel, they'll have a strong enough political structure in the countryside to push Thieu out of power by combined military and political efforts. It is a matter of time and logic since without American help the South cannot—as can the North—remain united politically.

I find this surprising coming from a Vietnamese who works for Americans. An is shockingly blunt. His perceptions show an involved yet deadly realistic mind. As we finish, An says he lived in southern California for a while during the fifties and attended journalism school. He looks at me.

"I have lived in peace," he says without emotion, "only two years of my life."

He wants the war to end. Yet, he knows he will probably have to live under Communism. It is hardly a pleasant prospect for a man accustomed to drinking coffee in French cafés and the relative freedom of working in Western journalism. I glance across the table and try to imagine for a moment how he feels about his life and his future. He lifts a teacup and looks past me as he drinks and doors close and I see nothing.

The GI

He'd started drinking that morning, and his eyes were glazed and focused on other places as he approached my table in a seamy little café on Tu Do Street named Jimmy's Kitchen.

"Mister," he grinned, angling his bony frame over the table, "I'm leaving Viet Nam and I'd like to buy you a drink." I motioned for him to sit down, though I had wanted to be alone.

He was tall and sunburned, a little slow, and as he wrapped his long fingers around a rum and coke I could see warring emotions in his face.

For he'd been in Viet Nam more than thirty-three months, extending his tour time and again for reasons he couldn't explain today, and in the end he had little to show for it except a recruiting sergeant's promise that "career army" on his identification papers would help finance a used car in Chicago.

"That helps, you know," he said, looking across the table with enlarged eyes. "The career army—that's a respected thing." Sure, buddy, I was thinking. In your world, anyway.

He was twenty-one, and he'd made a few friends here. He'd been busted once for drinking on duty and a three-inch scar on his forehead testified to the night he'd gotten in a street fight, again drunk.

He'd worked as a combat engineer, a security guard, a clerk, an information specialist and a mechanic, and like so many people who've come to Viet Nam he both loved and hated it. I began to like him as he talked on. He generated energy in his drunken, weary way that was hard to resist. And he knew things I didn't know yet.

He had strong feelings about the country, but he found

them hard to explain. "I don't think we should have gotten in," he mumbled while the bar girl came over to light a cigarette he'd been fumbling with. "But we've gone beyond the point where you can argue that anymore. I don't care what the people back home say, we're not getting out of here."

Wiser men might argue the point. But this soldier whose name happened to be Bill Miller hadn't been to the American embassy or the presidential palace or MACV headquarters. He'd spent his time on security posts, in obscure offices, or in bars where the girls asked 400 piasters a drink (nearly $4 at the official rate) to keep him company.

In every case, he followed orders and did his job, and took pride in the fact that he followed orders so well. He was a "good army man" and that was more important to him than anything else.

I was thinking as he talked that people like this make war possible. Give Bill Miller a uniform and talk about his country, his God—then send him off. Yet I couldn't dislike him. For he was a lonely kid, vaguely at odds with the world around him, often rejected by it. He had friends, he insisted, but today he was drinking alone.

"I've got mixed emotions about leaving," he said, propping his dusty boots on a chair. "I care about these people. But I admit I've made money here, too. These people are taking 'Sam' but Sam's letting himself be taken."

He was serious now. "I can think of five friends who died here. Maybe they died for nothing. But if America leaves, it'll really be for nothing. I'm sorry for the people who died, but that's part of the game."

I wondered how he would feel about the "game" if he lost a leg—or his balls. But I didn't say anything, and he kept on talking. I wanted him to keep on talking, too, for Viet Nam was still inside, and he wanted to get it out and put it behind him.

So we talked for a while and had another drink, and finally he smiled, showing discolored teeth almost green enough to match his sweaty fatigues. "I've been here too long," he said. "I'm going to miss my friends, but I've got to get back and make sure my roots are still there, at home, you know?"

I said I figured they were and we shook hands. I left him in Jimmy's nodding at his drink, I hoped a little closer to home.

Darkness

Something woke me. The shutters were rattling hard, and no wind or noise came through them to explain why. They clattered for half a minute, then stopped. Then they rattled again, filling the darkness with shivering.

I stumbled out of bed and groped downstairs to check the front door lock. Solid. Then to the open area where the maid washes clothes. Nothing. Only emptiness—and I stand in the black, colorless night waiting a moment more, watching and listening.

Now it is quiet and I move back to the bedroom, falling into uneasy sleep as early morning light touches the shutters in finger-thin shafts. I have a thing about Viet Nam. There is death outside and someone is always trying to explain why. But the dying continues and you keep wondering why, and soon you want answers for everything that is dark or forbidding, strange or nearby, and the answers never come.

The trembling shutters, a friend said next day, were caused by a B-52 strike, probably fifteen miles out of town. The planes flew in from Guam and dropped their cargo by electronic reckoning. Somewhere below people died in bunkers and caves, and in Saigon the concussion quietly rattled a few windows and awoke a few people.

Tina

April 21

She was short and solidly built, with charcoal eyes and long black hair. She sang Beatles songs with a gravelly little girl's voice when they came on the jukebox and laughed loudly at her own jokes. Then she would curse and poke at you if she got bored.

I met her the way any GI finds a woman in Saigon's bars. You walk in and she takes your arm in the darkness and you've got three minutes to buy her a tumbler of cold tea. If not, she's gone—no apologies and an abrupt farewell.

Tina came on stronger. She wore a photoflash-red mini that pushed her breasts nearly out of their cleavage and before you could say yes or no she was bouncing on your lap, singing songs and asking for a drink. The act cost me 4000 piasters—about $10 at street money-changing rates—before I could gather my wits. But it was my first time with a woman in a Saigon bar; the money was tuition. After an hour or so, broke but thoroughly entertained, I left.

The following night I was barely inside the bar—they are dark, like tunnels or swamps—when she appeared, tugging at my sleeve and looking up.

I'd done some homework. Experienced friends said to be pleasant but firm. Buy one "tea"—colored water the bars serve as a drink substitute—and see that she takes time to drink it. Don't buy her alcohol; it costs twice as much. Alcohol limits her effectiveness as a hustler, so the bar charges more per drink. She makes at least 100,000 piasters a month—about $250 street value, nearly $1000 at official rates—which is more than most generals are paid. Most of it is out of "tea" commissions; she gets half the price of anything you buy.

If you want to take her home, make the proposition after the first drink. Get a quick answer and be specific about the terms. It usually costs to take her out—to compensate for profits the bar will lose—then an equal sum for her afterward. If she likes you after all this, she'll lower the price, maybe meet you off hours.

Another rule: she'll be jealous. Don't let her see you hustle other girls. Proof of her loyalty is that she leaves whomever she's drinking with when you appear. If that seems less than romantic, Viet Nam has been at war for more than twenty years. The girls have seen a lot of men come and go. Nothing talks love better than money now.

So I tried all this on Tina, and wonder of wonders it worked. After two teas and an hour's talk, she scribbled her address on a scrap of paper. I hopped a Honda taxi and found her waiting at the door. Now that we'd left the bar behind, she was warm and pleasant. I couldn't help but like her. Once during the evening she showed me a drawerful of pictures, mostly family snapshots, of herself and friends.

From what I'd been told, I had a girl friend, Saigon style. I was naïve enough to believe this and lonely enough to want it to be true.

I went back to the bar the next night. I wasn't inclined to pay for another evening out so soon, but I assumed Tina would have tea with me and we would talk. She hugged me and ordered drinks. But then she left "for a few minutes." She came back, ordered another drink (before I could object that she hadn't finished the first), and left again.

She returned again and borrowed my pen to write some numbers on a scrap of paper. Then she kissed me quickly, mumbled something and walked over to the far end of the dark bar, giving the paper to a crew-cut American sitting on a bar stool.

I didn't go back for a few nights, and when I did, I told Tina to get her drinks somewhere else. She looked at me for a moment, said she was "sorry" and walked away.

2

As a New Yorker, Cambodia always seemed like the Land of Oz to me, a sugar and spice dateline mixed oddly among blood and thunder war stories filed out of Saigon. Fairy-tale writings of Sihanouk entertaining Jackie Kennedy, tourists and temples. Occasionally a navy riverboat took a wrong turn at some river junction and its crew briefly became POWs, of course, and the Pentagon advised us repeatedly that Cambodia's border areas were filled with Vietcong sanctuaries.

But Southeast Asia was a mystery to my Western mind, and I couldn't focus on Cambodia. Fat little Sihanouk in his white suits, women in wraparound dresses. Angkor Wat and elephants—and the Vietcong at rest? Nothing so upbeat could be fifty miles from Saigon.

Now, three weeks after arriving in Asia, I was assigned to take a turn covering the new war. Already, journalists had been captured. The Vietcong would soon control half the countryside. And Americans were readying to plunge across its border. The coup d'etat dislodging Sihanouk had unleashed energy in all Indochina—shock waves pushing flesh and fire across borders and stirring ancient ghosts in the trees and rice fields. I would be part of this soon.

Never-Never Land

Phnom Penh is a thirty-minute flight from Saigon, and everything seems clean and bright on the way, paddy fields and shiny temples blinking in the sun as we arc toward the runway. A line of ancient MIGs stands off to one side. Otherwise the airport carries no hint of war.

I pick a driver from the usual airport hustlers outside customs, and we go into the capital city. The war begins to show itself. Palm trees are standing in rings of barbed wire. The avenues, broad and lined with leafy trees, are sandbagged at the curbs with soldiers posted at regular intervals. Tempting dark-skinned girls drift past on cyclos. The city is stately, yet soft and pleasant at first glance, even in war.

There is an odd community of journalists around the pool of the Hotel Royale, a decaying Colonial monument of high-ceilinged hallways and flower gardens, which has become a center of communication. They don't seem to know anything, and it is catching. Living with a big and dangerous story, they are wary of each other, almost hostile. The man I'm replacing briefs me reluctantly and answers few of my questions. Then he tells me to go back to Saigon. It's *his* story, he insists.

It takes all day to iron this out, but he finally goes— destroying in the process what journalism school illusions I had left about camaraderie-in-the-ranks. I arrived in Asia, I admit, with an overload of pink-cheeked notions about deadlines, hard drinking, and friendships formed under war pressure. But this guy was mean as hell, and the others around the pool nearly match him. I get started by myself.

The usual process is to check in at local embassies, look at maps, learn names, talk to other reporters. I always thought in journalism school, too, that the story would be easy to find in a storm like this. Yet Phnom Penh looks like a resort town with barbed wire at the corners. The war isn't here. Nor is any solid information, except the kind that bureaucrats who know very little themselves pass on to reporters.

There are plenty of rumors. The city is about to fall, the government is in trouble, the American embassy is *really* running things. American soldiers are coming, Sihanouk will set up a jungle government. Worse yet, the military briefings are in French, and the American embassy people are vague and have no news.

You have to drive to the battles in private cars, and the threat of capture hangs over each trip. No military protection, like in Viet Nam. Men have already been lost, and people around the pool talk about who will be next.

One car of reporters returns to the hotel with a wide-eyed tale of ambush. They passed a squad of Vietcong who opened fire and nearly trapped them. The driver made a panicked U-turn and drove back through the bullets to get home. I feel everybody's fear as we talk, and the thought of going out there—the first time in any war—leaves me limp. I'm very, very afraid.

Messages from Washington

April 30

I should be charging around the countryside, ducking bullets and getting the *feel* of these historic moments. But I haven't moved anywhere. A newsmagazine doesn't require constant front-line work. My presence is needed only at crucial moments, turning points, battles of significance. The rest is news-of-the-moment, the territory of daily newspapers and wire services.

The problem, then, is when to go out. It is easy enough to talk to diplomats and military sources—liars though they may be—in Phnom Penh. It is often more productive. But then comes the crunch: am I a coward? Am I missing the color and action of really *good* journalism? At suppertime, reporters who've been out tell of near misses and impressions, and I feel like someone's little brother who isn't old enough to go out on dates.

And there is the machismo factor. Grown-up men in wartime (I'll soon join this silly fraternity) always measure each other in terms of the risks they take. If you haven't been to the "front" you can't write about the war. And like all clichés, there is some truth to this. You can't write about Harlem from Madison Avenue, and you can't write about Cambodia's war entirely from Phnom Penh; and so I am waiting for a "significant" battle to force me into the field, out from under my umbrella of fear.

Meanwhile, the Nixon administration has arranged quite a thunderstorm. Thousands of American troops have crossed the Cambodian border to raid Vietcong sanctuaries. It is the biggest news in the world this week and, ironically, I can't cover it. The Vietcong control the countryside between the capital and the Cambodian border. Driving in that direction would be suicide. I'll be expected to get reaction from the Cambodian government, and as usual they have almost nothing to say. Nixon didn't say he was coming, and they are somewhat embarrassed about the whole thing.

As it happens, I'm also in bed with a strep throat and a 104-degree temperature. And sleepy. I caught it somewhere between a warm rainstorm the other night and the hotel's arctic air-conditioning. A pretty poor showing, considering the occasion.

Messages from Home

May 1

The strep throat cuts like a wire collar. Fortunately, our Singapore man hit town a few days ago, so he can send the messages from this side of the war. The bedside radio says that American troops are doing well in the "parrot's beak," a piece of border area that pushes into Viet Nam's midsection. You can't tell much from Phnom Penh. Radio news bubbles and pops around the rock 'n' roll, but there is nothing to hold on to.

The Cambodian headlines suddenly shift to Ohio as I sit propped up on the hotel bed. At Kent State, four students have died for protesting the invasion, shot dead by National Guardsmen. There is rage and bitterness on all sides, and day by day I am thinking how this war strips away my country's sheen. We are so often what we say we are above. We seem intolerant, prone to violence, unable to learn from our mistakes. Instead of withdrawing from Viet Nam, we push into Cambodia. Instead of listening to students, we shoot them.

That's simplistic, I suppose. But American rhetoric insists we are a noble and humanitarian people, and the war says otherwise. Perhaps there are lessons being learned today: that we must confront ourselves and honestly measure our lust, finding ways to check it. I hope so, but I don't really believe it.

Scenes

May 5

. . . Beside the Royale Hotel swimming pool, a chubby platinum-coiffed matron poses other tourists—a fat man in Bermuda shorts and a middle-aged lady in a knee-length dress—beside a poster showing fighting and urging Cambodians to drive out the invaders and "proclaim the Republic." She snaps the Kodak Instamatic, complete with revolving flash cubes, and commands her friends to smile, which they do.

. . . At one of Phnom Penh's larger markets, a fruit vendor mumbles the Khmer equivalent of OK when I ask how he likes the new government. He can't get pears now, because shipping has been stopped by the war, and besides few people are shopping these days. They are off to war, and as a result he and other vendors have had to lower prices.

. . . I walk a lot now, talking to people in shops, interviewing diplomats, making the rounds of bars, letting wheels work inside me: still trying to work out the culture shock of confronting war, my fear of dying. I smoked opium last night. Somewhere in the smoke, my body turning to putty and melting under mama-san's hard caress during a back rub, I reached into the recesses of my mind and measured the wedge working to separate fear from the sure knowledge that soon I have to drive the country roads where journalists are disappearing. I'm coming around, slowly.

. . . South of the capital, a battle is sputtering at Ang Tasom, I'm told. The Vietcong blew up a bridge nine kilometers this side of the town. When that happened, a Cambodian colonel hurried over. Twenty-four hours later, he asked some journalists to carry a message to headquarters asking for a bulldozer. The bulldozer arrived and the bridge was repaired. Meanwhile the Cambodians were ambushed, so the colonel hired four cyclo drivers at two dollars each to haul ammunition from Ang Tasom to his position at the bridge. It is hard to tell what happened after that. Communications are difficult. The colonel's radio is thirty years old.

. . . At the Palais Governmental, Cambodia's foreign minister toasts the twelve-man South Vietnamese delegation with champagne. He promises his country will make every effort to help Vietnamese refugees. But formal discussions haven't begun. These take time, though his army's racist slaughter of ethnic Vietnamese has been the center of worldwide attention for weeks. For the moment, the Cambodian government agrees "in principle" to allow extra planes in to carry out refugees. But that and other things must be talked about further. And there are only two clerks to process two thousand exit visas thus far granted to Vietnamese refugees. So, little has been accomplished. Meanwhile, the group dines on fish with mushrooms, steak, soup, Caesar salad, ice cream with fruit, and French pastry.

. . . I visit one of the Catholic churches where Vietnamese are "detained." The menu is simpler. Refugee women squat by cooking pots, stirring fish heads and vegetables over smoky fires. They turn to watch me without expression as I walk by. Men with nothing to do hunker down in long rows against the buildings like crows on a fence. About fifty people are jammed into one fifteen-by-fifteen-foot room: babies asleep, slender teenage girls, old crones with sunken eyes. A gray-suited Cambodian official and an equally gray Vietnamese emissary were here yesterday. The Cambodian told the people to blame Sihanouk for their troubles. The Vietnamese official offered them condolences and promised to do what he could.

. . . At a riverboat nightclub, the band plays "The Tennessee Waltz," and dark Khmer girls dance by my table as if nothing is happening outside the city. The one reminder of war is an occasional military uniform.

The cyclo driver who takes me there explains in halting English that "the people like Mr. Lon Nol because he is a hard worker." The driver adds: "Mr. Lon Nol has no wife [Sihanouk's wife, Monique, was unpopular] so he can give long hours to the Cambodian people. He works late at the office every night. He keeps the town clean, and he will keep the Vietcong out of our towns." The driver, a stringy little man, is talking in my ear over the handlebars as he peddles. "Sihanouk was selling our country to the Vietnamese. Lon Nol will not do that."

. . . The Cambodians are making little distinction now between Vietnamese and Vietcong. Most of them consider the war simply a Vietnamese invasion. At the morning military briefing, we are told again and again how Vietcong organize Vietnamese villagers. Documents show Vietnamese allegedly cooperating in arrests and executions of Cambodian provincial officials. Posters around town show Vietnamese fighting against Khmer (Cambodian) soldiers. One banner proclaims: "Cambodia for the Cambodians. The Vietnamese must go." There are about 600,000 Vietnamese in Cambodia (which is also called "Kampuchea") and that makes racism almost as big a problem as war. The ethnic hatreds are centuries old.

. . . I had dinner at an American diplomat's house last night. I talked to the Australian military attaché this morning. And as usual, I went to the morning military briefing. Then I had lunch with another reporter, trading a thought or two. Following that, I got out my swimsuit and spent an hour by the Hotel Royale pool. I was in a deck chair, in fact, when some television reporters returned from the countryside. Nothing unusual out there, they said. But I looked at the chair and saw vines growing out of it, clinging to my arms and legs. I came to Cambodia as green as those vines, but I am about to cut them away and emerge from the fog of hesitation, fear of the unknown and inertia I feel and go to the field. I see it coming and I feel a little shaky still. But I also feel good about this. Understand?

Firefight

All week the word is that Neak Luong, a river town and ferry crossing thirty-six miles south of the capital, will be the next big battle. I am resolved to go—convinced now that it is time to test myself. Fear has given way to restlessness, and restlessness to realism. I have to get off my ass or go home.

The highway down to Neak Luong is narrow blacktop. At this writing, I've driven it three times. On each trip the last miles were terrifying, for we passed through heavy groves of mango and banana trees with no way to see behind them. Each car had several reporters, and we'd stop and talk periodically to peasants walking near the road. "VC, monsieur?" and we'd point south. We hoped the people would say something if there was trouble.

Today is Thursday. The Vietcong took Neak Luong last Sunday. Cambodian units are supposed to link up this coming Monday with American and South Vietnamese troops at the ferry crossing, so the government wants it back. Unfortunately, the Cambodians were badly scattered—one officer says his men are "lost"—and now the Vietcong have moved even closer to Phnom Penh, about nine miles north of the river crossing.

Today, several of us reach government lines about noon. It is warm and sticky and my shirt is already soaked. There is a shapeless hole in the road, fifteen feet across and about six deep, which VC combat engineers blasted out during the night. The trucks can't get around it and so soldiers are filling the space with rocks and dirt, hauling them from the fields in wicker baskets.

The government plans a big offensive: twenty-four hundred troops, backed by trucks waiting along the road

29

filled with rifles, bullets, mortars, rockets and machine guns. The men are positioned across the countryside in a long crow's wing. Tanks lead the forward elements through orchards, fields and jungle. Three tanks, two hundred yards apart, are protecting the highway—lumpish metal hulks in a sea of soldiers' faces.

Some Cambodians are shouting now. They've seen half a dozen Vietcong a thousand yards away, and running east. The soldiers shoot mortars at them which explode in distant thumps and clouds of smoke.

Other soldiers don't even notice. They are busy taking fruit, vegetables, and chickens from the farmhouses. One group sits under a tree in one farmer's yard eating his pears and potatoes. One little man, grinning like a weasel, grabs a squawking hen and ties her legs to his backpack. The hen struggles briefly, then stares blankly at the world upside down, bouncing as he walks.

The procession moves slowly: tanks, troops, journalists, two fully equipped three-man television teams hooked together by wire. A few reporters are walking "point," fifty yards ahead of the lead tank. I'm two hundred yards behind that tank, which seems reasonably safe. Photographer Bob Richards, a black man built like a football guard, has "premonitions" we ought to drop back further.

"How do you feel?" he asks, looking down.

"I'm OK." I am excited, frightened and feeling good like a kid driving too fast in a new car. If I am in trouble, I don't know it. "How are you?"

"It's coming, man. It's coming"—and he is right.

One second the countryside is calm: trucks and tanks grinding slowly, soldiers talking, birds chirping. Then the jungle ahead explodes. The line has walked into an ambush. The next minute is confused. Everyone is shouting and the air is splitting with noise. Bob and I dive behind a thick tree. A sniper is firing up the road— just enough to pin us down. He seems far away and I feel oddly relieved that the bullets whistle as they go past; somehow I assume this shows that they are losing momentum.

The reporters walking point are trapped. They have snipers on each side and Cambodians firing all around. No one is hurt, luckily, but when they reach our tree later one TV man has lost his pants crawling frantically around. Others are cut up and covered with mud from diving in and out of holes.

Bob and I settle down. Sniper rounds come in whistling low on the left. So we inch to the right. And vice versa. Fortunately, the VC trooper usually fires on one side or the other. He seems to be firing randomly, clipping a branch here and there, but not shooting directly at us.

The rifle rounds snap viciously through the trees. Down the road, machine-gun bursts follow. Then the heavy thumping of mortar fire. Then the tanks open up and prolonged booming drowns out everything else. Cambodians shout a lot when they fight, and you can hear them yelling between the bursts, bangs and thunder.

This is my first time under fire. I figure I ought to think about it. But at first nothing comes to mind. The tree has big branches, and since lying on my back is the safest position, I spend most of the battle staring at clouds: big puffy ones. They remind me of grade school summers in Michigan. I shift to my stomach. Thorns scratch my arms, and ants and spiders crawl out from under the leaves. An Indian cameraman from a tree behind us comes over to offer water and make conversation. A sniper's bullet cuts a sprig where he was standing, and it falls like a green feather to the ground.

The fire keeps rolling out of the jungle in short—then bunched up—bursts. Smoke rises from homes the soldiers are burning—the owner's penalty for letting VC spend the night. Every few minutes a bullet whistles by our tree. That sniper hasn't forgotten us. He is a messenger, I am thinking, from a man whose shadow sometimes shakes you awake, frightened, from the beginnings of sleep; always there, unexplained.

I shake off this idea and try to think about war again. All I decide is that decisions about it—moral, political or whatever—have little to do with actually being fired at.

The reality here is pain; bullets, blood, farmers burned out, lives given up in death or lost years. People who say war is necessary ought to be here. Get mud on their clothes. Watch someone die.

My mind shuts off. Something inside me refuses to deal with this anymore. I look at Bob. He looks at me. We are both waiting for this to end.

The firing has stopped, and we begin running low toward our cars. I see a dead man lying below an embankment, shot through the head. You can see only a little of his face. It is covered with a bloody bandage and death has altered what is left to the look of a skull. He was a young man, now lying on his back in death, arms and legs spread-eagle.

A television crew starts filming a voice-over using him as a backdrop. The correspondent kneels beside him, holding his microphone and looking sternly at the camera. Then he tells his audience what happened today. They will see the body, and him. Perhaps the soundman will pick up a few sniper rounds still being fired in the distance.

As I walk away, more rounds whistle overhead, perhaps twenty feet up. They keep coming in as I try to walk away from that dead man and the war. We reach the car and tell our driver, San, who has been waiting all this time, to drive like hell for Phnom Penh. That's fine with him and it is fine with me.

Thank You, Mr. President

Nearly midnight and the bars will close soon. A long day's work leads to thoughts of a drink or two, maybe a girl. Phom Penh women are plentiful butterflies, and they are cheap. And they come on wheels.

Ride down one of the city's leafy avenues in the evening, past the strategic points. Cyclo bells signal the chase. Girls on the sidewalk jump into bicycle carts driven by bony taxi drivers: Indians overtaking a covered wagon.

"Bon soir, monsieur," purrs one. "I love you," offers another. They keep pace for a block or so while you decide. They'll bargain in the rain if the price is right, leap into your cyclo if you seem shy. But the sales pitch is gentle, for Phom Penh at night is hushed, like countryside at twilight, and the girls are part of this: gecko lizards chirping, birds trilling, soft grinding of cyclos along darkened streets, an occasional car.

Tonight I am tired and in no mood for the cyclo girls. A drink, perhaps; nothing more. I try a quiet bar near the river. A few girls are inside, most of them unexciting. One is tall, thin, very dark, tempting. She is young. A wicked smile, shiny teeth. I resolve to drink quietly and get a good night's sleep, but we flirt.

She begins playing peek-a-boo and I try halfheartedly to ignore her: a button unbuttoned, the sarong untied slightly, an invitation to pinch this, pat that. Fatigue, for the moment, wins. I turn to my drink; she moves away, scowling a little.

A Cambodian sits down several stools away, perhaps fifty, looking lean in military khaki. When the girl leaves he asks, in French, if I am American. He wants to know America's reaction to Nixon's move. He is a National

Police official, obviously a ranking one: dark, losing his crew cut to old age, leathery, wears glasses. But he seems sincerely curious, not belligerent, and he is reasonably sober.

So I tell him in broken French that the country is divided, that some are terribly angry, particularly the young. I add, because it is true and because I do not know what this man believes in, that many Americans approved of the war effort, perhaps still do; that many supported the move.

The conversation is labored, perhaps half understood, lubricated by the cognacs he continues to buy. Between the third and fourth drink, I think, the girl returns. The conversation must *sound* interesting even though she can't understand it. She hooks a long thin arm through mine and pretends to listen, flirting a little during each pause. The police official glances at her, then we look at each other, and suddenly he is reaching for his wallet.

"You must understand how grateful we are," he slurs, lifting out a five-hundred-riel note and waving it before the girl. "The Americans have saved Kampuchea from communism and we can never repay our debt to you." He looks at the girl, who looks at me and smiles. "Take her, with my thanks to your country."

He gives the mama-san money and I protest, but not too strongly, and the girl flashes that wicked smile again.

So now we shake hands and I promise to buy him a drink one of these nights and I call a cyclo. I guess I owe this one to Richard Milhous Nixon, though I'm not sure he'd understand. The night is silent as we ride through the streets and the girl sits on my lap, giggling.

Exodus

All morning I stood on the deck watching refugees climb out of crowded buses and clamber across wooden gang-planks to the ship's deck. It was hot, though a wind stirred off the river briefly as sailors carried the old or crippled people on board. The breeze tilted against the stick figures of old women, mouths black from years of chewing betel nut, standing in groups on the dock and jabbering excitedly. Younger women, not so noisy, leaned under loads of pots and pans and babies, squatting on wicker mats to suckle the youngest children as their husbands claimed campsites.

By midmorning, the metal deck had become a small city of tents and cooking fires. Children run everywhere. The air smells gamy like the Saigon market. Families construct half shelters by tying blankets and wicker mats to a cable stretched across the center of the deck. These are scattered like playing cards in the first heavy wind after the ship gets underway. But they keep tying these temporary homes together again, just as they are re-working their lives.

I'm doing a story about the trip, playing vulture again. Another tale of people suffering—copy that makes me wither inside. I sometimes think my colleagues and I go from graveyard to graveyard unable to decide who is more important, the living or the dead. And we like it— or we wouldn't be here.

Squealing, fussing packs of kids stand around like armies of pygmies, clutching cans of C rations or dipping dirty fingers into bowls of rice and fish made into gruel with canned milk and cooking oil. Down in the hold, a thousand refugees have an identical community, no tents needed. But for them the air is rancid, diluted only slightly by fans. Bad smells are the price of protection from the rain.

This is the command ship, the *Vung Tau,* a four thousand-ton tank carrier which came to Phnom Penh two days ago carrying fifty tons of food, medicine and clothing. Weeks of wordy negotiations between well-fed politicians preceded the move. Because the Vietcong controlled parts of the river on the way up, the fleet was increased from twenty to forty ships, half gunboats. About ten thousand people are leaving Cambodia today.

Shortly after midday, we move away from the docks. The engines make a whooshing and grinding sound. Monks in orange robes wave from across the river, and we pass Sihanouk's gold-tiled palace, now closed, off to starboard as the city slips away. The first of several rainstorms sweeps across the deck within minutes, driving mothers and kids under blankets and mats that are falling down all over the place. The Asian capacity to endure discomfort is amazing. I wonder as I watch if I could be that tough. Some families eat dinner in the rain. Others wash clothes. Still others just sit: nothing to do but sit and take it.

The afternoon throws three storms at them. Everyone from the tiniest naked toddler to the most wizened old man grabs a broom, shoes, anything that will push water. They channel the muddy streams into low spots, using the brooms and the rubber sandals as water wedges. Then they scoop the water into buckets and dump it over the side. The little kids are slopping around in the water and laughing, like this is some great mudhole. The glee is heartwarming to watch. One tiny kid squats in a puddle and slaps his rubber sandal up and down, shrieking with delight while people around him scurry away from the spray.

As the day fades, sailors check the water supply and carry sewage away. Then darkness settles over the deck, pricked by the red points of cigarettes glowing in the tent city and ruffled occasionally by the cries of children.

I find a sailor who speaks both English and Vietnamese, and we go down to the hold.

I have to talk to people, get names and quotations, ask how they feel. It is hard. These Vietnamese have lost a rare chance to live in peace. Now, whole families are homeless. Relatives have died, and many refugees have no place to go. So how do you feel, Mister? I'm always amazed when someone honestly answers a question like that.

We approach a young father, barefoot and wearing boxer shorts, crowded into a wicker mat with his wife and kids. He was a house painter. He says the Cambodian soldiers told him to get back to Viet Nam—"or they would kill us." He is lying on his side as he talks, listless; worried because he has no relatives in Viet Nam. There are five children, who watch as we talk. Like most of the urban-raised refugees, the family will migrate to one of South Viet Nam's cities, which are already full of homeless people.

The sailor and I talk next to an old woman lying on a mat. She waves her hands around and describes how her father was shot by Cambodian soldiers. Nearby, a twenty-year-old girl, dark and painfully attractive, won't talk to us. The sailor speaks to her mother. She says the girl's fiancé disappeared. She thinks he is in prison. It is more likely, I am thinking, that he is dead. They will go to Saigon and I am wondering as we talk if I'll see her in a bar. She has a beautiful face, and the bars are the only place she can make enough money to live well: another Tina.

I go upstairs, open some C rations and fruit, and sleep fitfully on a sailor's bunk for a few hours. Somebody tells me before I drop off that two babies have been born and one woman has started labor since we left Phnom Penh. Just before sunrise, the fleet drops anchor across the border near a town called Hong Ngu. About 5:00 A.M. we begin moving toward shore.

A pink sunrise is threading its way through the treetops. I'm on deck, curious how the Vietnamese will react to seeing their homeland. I expect people will be at the railing, talking; maybe pointing at the town. Nothing. Business as usual. A woman washes clothes while a naked kid screams and grabs at her blouse. Men are packing the night's bedding. Fish and rice simmer on charcoal pots. Maybe a dozen people watch as we approach shore. Everyone else is packing silently, as if nothing unusual is happening.

The ship nudges the muddy riverbank and people carry the baggage of their former lives ashore. A refugee official is reading instructions into a microphone in the village square. There are tables for medical help, forms for police records and for rice rations. Village girls in white *ao dais* stand around to help, and vendors sell iced tea and Cokes.

They will get tents to live in and fifty grams of rice per person each day. There will be cooking oil, canned milk, dried fish and other things, like money to travel to other parts of Viet Nam. Twenty-three thousand refugees have come out of Cambodia so far, and thousands more are on the move.

And life, for whatever it is worth, goes on. A half-blind widow named Nguyen Thi Mai whose hair was falling out from a scalp disease told me on the ship that life looked good to her. "I am very, very happy to go back to Viet Nam," she smiled, "and I am happy not to be killed." Mrs. Nguyen must know something that I don't, I am thinking. A smile like that deserves plenty of rice and a lot of good living, and I hope she finds them in her new home.

3

I catch a ride out of Hong Ngu on a navy riverboat. The men have tape recorders and steaks and girlie magazines aboard—and a Vietnamese crew sleeping in the hold. As part of Vietnamization, the Asian crew will soon take control of the boat. "It's like giving a Cadillac to a bunch of kids," grumps one sailor, waving his hand at the boyish-looking Vietnamese. But he also has a letter from home and he wants to be there.

My month in Phnom Penh is over, and it is time to report again from Viet Nam. Despite nearly two months in Asia, the war remains a blurred image, a hazy chart of spots and arrows and conflicting orders from Washington, Hanoi, Saigon and now Phnom Penh. I have no feeling for the totality of it. As the boat moves along the Delta River, I keep hoping that something will happen to make this conflict easier to understand: write about, think about, live with. It never happens, though.

First Aid, American Style

May 25

I am in Chau Duc, a tiny Delta town on Cambodia's border, looking for stories. The Vietnamese are fighting across the border, using the town as a field headquarters. The city has a smelly market that makes my eyes water, but no hotel, so a photographer named Hugh Van Es and I try the local navy Seabee headquarters.

It is an old French prison, walls three feet thick. I see shattered plaster and pockmarks where bullets and B-40 rockets slammed into the walls during Tet 1968. The sailors are friendly. We get bunks and an invitation to watch the nighttime movie in the bar. Drinks are cheap though the men are boring. We seem to be at Joe's Bar & Grill in Chau Duc: baseball scores, the wife and kids, fast cars. But the men want to talk. They know Hugh and I get around, and they are curious about other parts of Viet Nam.

Yet it isn't the bar that makes the night. The Navy has an emergency medical clinic here. An hour short of midnight we hear chopper blades. Everyone rushes outside. Hugh and I help carry stretchers and we take wounded Vietnamese marines off the hovering helicopters, which kick up dust and blink crimson night-lights and make so much clatter you can't hear above them.

We give the men cigarettes and lay them out in lines of stretchers along a corridor while a doctor and his medical corpsmen do the bloody things that doctors do. I feel good helping these men in tiger suits, cut up in a war they can't escape. Then one of the Seabees leans over to say something.

"We fix these Vietnamese pretty regularly," he confides in a low voice, looking at the ground. "But it's a job . . ."

I am looking at a man behind him lying on a stretcher, bleeding through his pants.

". . . When we get Americans in here, things really jump. It's a lot different, you know what I mean?"

"Yeah." And I look away so he can't see my face.

Death and Diplomacy

May 26

I am sitting in the Chau Duc officers' mess, a large tent, with the local ARVN commander's chief aide, a young captain. He is American educated, sharp and cynical, and talkative. We are talking about the Cambodian campaign. I mention I rode out of Phnom Penh a few weeks ago with the Vietnamese navy on a refugee mission. He smiles oddly, looks at me a moment, then tells me a story.

About a month ago, the Vietnamese mission in Phnom Penh called a press conference to protest the death of a navy corporal. He'd come to town with the fleet to carry out refugees, and he and two other sailors went into town that day. Around midnight they were attacked by a gang of Cambodians on Norodom Street, dragged into a deserted schoolhouse and beaten. The corporal was stabbed to death.

The Cambodians were embarrassed. Their army's atrocities in the countryside a few months earlier were still in everyone's mind. So they broadcast an official apology within hours, promising payments to the sailor's relatives.

Reporters, in turn, filled the telegraph office with stories of razor-edge tensions between the two countries. Everyone wondered how the incident would affect the two countries' diplomatic and military relations. I remembered the incident as the captain told it, and I had been ready that week to suggest a story to New York if a bigger feud developed.

But it was all a sham. The captain laughs as he takes another pull on a bottle of Vietnamese beer, and says that the corporal and his friends were caught smuggling by some Cambodian hoods and taken out of action gangland style.

"They were smuggling and they deserved to be killed," he adds with a shrug. "The problem was that the Cambodian government needed Vietnamese military aid. So the government apologized."

I smile, too, wondering what other stories I've been missing lately.

A Friend

I was standing in the lobby of Phnom Penh's Royale Hotel when he approached: owlish glasses, bushy black moustache, big smile, hand shooting out to shake mine, a genuinely friendly man unlike most reporters in this tense town.

"I'm Jerry Miller from CBS," said the enthusiastic voice. "Just got in . . . confusing isn't it?"

I agreed and offered to brief him on local problems. At lunch we talked a long time about Cambodia. I found myself liking this man for his lack of pretension, his curiosity and willingness to share, also, what *he* knew. He was a seasoned wire service reporter and had worked for years in Rome. Now he had come to Cambodia for CBS—his first time in Asia.

He was a "producer"—a program director for a camera crew. He enjoyed talking about stories he was doing. He'd trade information if you weren't competing with him (I wasn't) and, most important to me at least, he was always open. I felt I could trust him, and I felt he respected me in return.

Jerry and I talked regularly, sometimes trading intelligence. We also ranged into the problems of Africa (he worked in Biafra for a while), American politics and sometimes the journalism trade—our lives and how they moved to a rhythm that wives or girl friends rarely understood, and how costly that could be. One time Jerry pulled up behind me in his car honking loudly. I got out and listened to a mile-a-minute account of the murder of the previously-mentioned Vietnamese sailor. I wouldn't have heard about it for hours otherwise.

We said good-bye a few days after that and I left Cambodia. I really didn't know him deeply, but I was grateful that our lives had touched briefly. I felt warmed by this.

A few weeks later Jerry got into a jeep with George Syvertsen, a CBS correspondent, and Ramnik Lekhi, an Indian cameraman, and drove toward the town of Takeo. A small battle had been fought there. News reports later said the three stopped at a government checkpoint about halfway down. They were warned by Cambodian soldiers not to go farther.

They didn't have to go. Takeo wasn't worth it. An American diplomat once berated me during an interview for the trouble journalists cause by taking chances. Why do we *do* it, he asked heatedly? I could only tell him you always feel driven to find the center of things— a vision around some corner that will make everything fall into place. If there are risks, you calculate the odds— and sometimes you go.

A few minutes later the Cambodians heard a loud explosion and several bursts of fire. Vietcong guerrillas had hit Jerry's jeep with a B-40 rocket. When soldiers finally reached the ruined jeep, it was empty. Jerry and the cameraman were found in shallow graves a few days later, both shot in the head. I think about the long talks now—that hand shaking mine and Jerry's smile and how he must have looked, for the earth covering him had turned to mud in the tropical rains, mocking all of us.

Death in Little Boxes

Clark called and said to catch a plane to Da Nang, fast. I was in bed, sleeping late I admit, and I cursed loudly at the telephone after I put it down. But reports reaching Saigon said that one hundred civilians had been killed in a Vietcong raid up north. It looked like the worst Communist atrocity since the mass killings in Hue during Tet 1968.

By the time I reached Da Nang it was too dark to drive to Thanh My, where it happened. I had a drink with a friend from AP who described things somewhat.

About eighteen miles south there are three hamlets clustered around a central market on Highway One. Most people in the area have relatives serving the Vietcong. But one hamlet, Thanh My, houses mostly families of local government officials.

It was dark and almost without a moon when the attack began. The mortars came first, some of them white phosphorus which set fire to the houses. In this area, where there is trouble regularly, people build bunkers, usually a hole in the ground covered by sheet metal and sandbags. Within minutes hundreds of families had fled underground.

Shortly after that two companies of Vietcong moved into the village. Mortar explosions continued, and they moved around under cover of them. One squad kept a small group of American marines pinned down on one side of town. Another briefly attacked some Vietnamese troops guarding a bridge.

Then sometime between 2:00 and 3:00 A.M. a group of sappers—elite troops trained in sabotage and killing people—entered Thanh My. The women and kids were still underground, but the Vietcong knew where to find them.

They went from house to house, throwing explosives inside the tiny bunkers.

I tried to imagine the horror of this: trapped in a small room and suddenly it is blowing to hell. You can't run and you are on fire, shoulder to shoulder, with people you love who are dying, too. There is no place even to crawl to. . . .

American helicopters arrived now, and the Vietcong split into four- and five-man groups to get out. The Americans found Thanh My in ashes and death. Next day, an old dwarf who survived showed reporters the charred hands of his twelve-year-old son, all that was left of the boy. They were wrapped in paper and he was weeping as he opened it.

The first thing I see when I arrive is a tiny red casket ringed by joss sticks and candles. This is for a kid named Nguyen Thanh. He was five. A concussion grenade killed his entire family. I look into the bunker, still smoking two days later. The black bricks surround an enclosure so small that Thanh's family had to be crouching against one another when the grenade came in. Neighbors stand around weeping, staring vacantly as I stop. There is nothing to say. I feel numb, immersed in an inkblot of tangled emotions at all of this blood and terror.

A marine lieutenant who fought the Vietcong briefly that night says that Thanh My was the prettiest hamlet he knew: neat rows of homes with trees and winding paths. As he talks, I am looking at a dead landscape of ashes, gutted buildings, blackened crockery, charred and twisted tools, and bicycles. There is a heavy smell of burned and rotting flesh.

Most of the dead are buried now. "It was wall-to-wall bodies," grunts the lieutenant. He is being tough and businesslike, but disgust and pain are all over his face. He gets me a translator and I ask an old man, gray and thin, what happened.

"When the V.C. came, they shot every house." He points to rows of blackened huts. "When the people ran, they shot them, too. They threw grenades into the bunkers." Somehow, the old man lived through the night. "I saw them and ran into my shelter," he says, but he doesn't know why they missed his house.

Another villager says the sappers called into some bunkers, telling people it was safe to come out and shooting them when they did.

I can watch a funeral just so long and something shuts off inside me. I want to keep death at a distance. Everyone does. And it isn't easy in Viet Nam, even as a journalist with a press card to shield you against the things you deal with. For people are dying all around you, and it seems that it is catching, like plague. Anyway, it is time to leave. Food and building materials have arrived from government offices, and a few carpenters are working now. As I start to walk away, my foot bumps against a piece of metal half buried in some ashes, and I stoop to pick it up. It is the tail of a mortar, gray and finny like the end of a metal fish. I put it in my pocket. Somehow I want to take a piece of Thanh My home.

A speckled midday sun reflects off mounds of ashes colored brown and black. A woman cooks fish over a small flame under a sheet-metal half shelter, and government officials walk about the ruins, writing on clipboards. Under another half shelter, two candles and some joss sticks burn for another funeral.

The marine lieutenant has a jeep, and we stop at his team house so I can get the name of a marine who died that night. Then I get in another jeep for the ride back to Da Nang. I feel a closed-up anger as though my body is a fist that I can't open and I don't talk to the driver on the way back.

Coming Out

Time stops in helicopters. You push through space jiving with the flop-flop rhythm and watching the distant earth, wondering occasionally if the blade above is about to stop rotating. My first time up I took a door seat without knowing the door stays open. We lifted off, and it was like straddling the edge of a cliff. The Vietnamese general taking us on a tour of his fire bases saw me stiffen and politely insisted we change seats. He treated me like a frightened kid in a whorehouse for the rest of the day.

We are flying to Cambodia's border. The first stop en route is a hill with a numbered name. Shirtless GIs, digging holes, stop to stare. As several passengers get off, my mind plays tricks with the scene. For a moment it is a work camp: windy, barren, filled with men who want to leave. Viet Nam has hundreds of mountain top fire bases. They aren't prison camps, but how do you explain rows of barbed wire, guns and searchlights to your subconscious?

We lift off. Our rotor wash raises an explosion of dust over the GIs, whose bodies are bent against it. They quickly go back to work against the calendar. Another thirty minutes of bumpy flight north through rising clouds. Then the jungle canopy splits to show a patch of earth stripped of green coloring. This is Firebase Exodus, a forward position for the scheduled American withdrawal from Cambodia.

Here the withdrawal began four days ago. Combat engineers climbed into helicopters at Firebase David six miles inside Cambodia and choppered to this spot, eight hundred yards on the Viet Nam side. The helicopters hovered and the men climbed down ropes into two bomb craters, called landing zones, cut earlier by two-thousand-pound bombs.

For seven hours they felled trees and cleared brush, widening the craters into a helicopter pad. Then they radioed David and a bigger chopper arrived carrying tents, maps, weapons and the forward elements of headquarters company.

The camp today is more than two hundred yards across and filled with teen-age soldiers. It was christened with a Bible quote, and I think immediately of Joan Baez singing "God Is on Our Side" at a Berkeley antiwar rally when some officer proudly tells me this.

It is an uncomfortable and dangerous place. Headquarters company, plus combat and engineering detachments, are here, while Alpha, Baker and Charlie companies will cross the river in a few days to meet Nixon's June 30 deadline, having walked and fought their way through Cambodian jungles to get out. Exodus is an expedient. The strategy is to have temporary firebases just over the border to cover withdrawals. Then the camp will be abandoned and the men returned to the Pacification work they were doing before the invasion.

Meanwhile they expect to take a few casualties. "We'll get hit," frowns one lieutenant, pointing at military maps in his tent while I wonder not-so-idly what it would be like to be overrun here. "One of these nights, the mortars and rockets are coming." The lieutenant, who looks like he should be studying engineering at Princeton, assumes the Vietcong will aim their rockets from across the river. And Exodus, with sandbag bunkers and a canvas headquarters tent, will have a rough time if they do.

I ask a sergeant, a combat engineer, if he expects the same. "Hell, yes," he shoots back, looking soldierlike with dog tags flopping over a bare chest, "that's why we build bunkers. They don't hit you for the first few days. They sit back and analyze the situation first."

As I look around, dirt-caked infantrymen move about the trash-covered camp, stringing wire, filling sandbags with red clay, clearing brush, digging holes. Through trees to the north you can see Cambodia. Every ten minutes or so a big helicopter carrying supplies clatters down, so convulsing the camp in its rotor wash that men have to hold the headquarters tent down to keep it from blowing away. Trash, equipment and newspapers sail around as if driven by hurricane winds.

Compared to Cambodia, however, Exodus looks good to the soldiers. "Viet Nam's an R & R spot by comparison," says one kid with blond hair. "It was rotten over there. One day we were taking so much fire that we couldn't get a chopper in with water. We had to catch rainwater with our ponchos. I'll take this place any day, no shit!"

My favorite character is Rance Lee, a tough teen-ager from Staten Island. Lean and dirty, he's hot to be interviewed and something of a Times Square cowboy. He wears love beads and looks both stoned and killer-trained at the same time, nodding a curly head as he talks, rocking to music I don't hear.

"I've seen enough action to last me a lifetime," he laughs, bitter and funny at once. "I wish I was back on the block, man, digging the city. Just trippin' back on Forty-second Street."

He laughs again and talks about how awful Cambodia was, slamming a machete into a wooden plank for emphasis. He talks about how he joined the army in patriotic fervor ("Wow, what a bummer!") and we promise to meet someday in The City.

"I had a beard like yours before I got into this mess," he calls out as I walk away. "Very cool." He waves again, "See you back there, man."

American Girl

I put an American girl on the plane to Hong Kong today, the first Western woman I'd been close to since leaving the United States. She wore dungarees and smiled a lot and she was finishing a long trip, chasing herself through Asia and running from the pain of lost love and confusion about her life in America. She was warm and ample, talkative and troubled during the days and nights we spent together. The sharing of deeply held doubts—vague, anguished feelings of insecurity, rootlessness and little feeling for the future except uncertain hope—brought us together and bound us temporarily, For a while, she wanted to stay; at least part of her did.

I wanted her to go, for our troubles and our passions were all we really shared; and they in turn would become burdens. So we moved carefully from the beginning to the end of our time, and at the airport it was all smiles and lighthearted exchanges. Nothing was solved in either of our lives, but no point in talking about it now.

Of course we promise to write. But when she is aboard the plane I say "that's done" almost in relief. One thing remains: the memory of common feelings and experiences that an Asian girl, however gentle, cannot easily provide. I love Asia now, but I am still a Western man. And being so, I miss that Western girl even though I didn't want her to stay.

4

Another month in Cambodia. The reporter's life can really be a drag. Thirty days in an Asian hotel is a long time, especially with no one around except other journalists, who can be boring as hell. You have dinner with sources, but that's work—interrogating someone and trying to be friendly about it. The bars are there. But you know why the girls talk to you, and you struggle to keep from spending too much money. Work again. Phnom Penh has opium dens. But what if the airport is attacked at 3:00 A.M. and I am strung out? And fear—plenty of it. The roads aren't any safer than the last time around. Nor has the Cambodian government become any more talkative.

I must stop this brooding. I go on like this until the entire world turns black. Asia, for me, is a place of extreme emotions, but they are mixed. So let us try to list happy things. The Royale pool is a fine diversion. The restaurants are good. The girls are pretty as ever, no matter what they cost. And the story is one of the world's best. Take my complaints as one side of this. Hard work, in fact, isn't the problem, nor fear. It is more personal than that—a loneliness that I can't fix, which might be just as bad in New York.

The Pilot

> Of course I don't like killing. But it's a job and I do it
> well and I'm proud that I do it well. They are trying to
> kill Americans, and I don't think they should be able
> to do that and I'm helping to stop them. I look at them
> as less than human, like animals. I have to do that. If
> I didn't do that, I could never go back to the states and
> live a normal life. But I'm glad to be able to kill them
> well, because it's my job. I'm trained for that, and I'm
> a pro.

I'm sitting upstairs in a huge house in Phnom Penh. It is
newly rented for the U.S. embassy's naval attaché. (Right.
We've added a naval attaché.) His furniture will come
from Bangkok soon. Meanwhile we are drinking bourbon
in wicker chairs and arguing about war. The naval attaché is a reasonable fellow—for a military man, at least—
but he's too drunk to keep with the conversation. We
started drinking earlier at a Fourth of July party and
ended up here.

The man proud of being able to kill so well sits across
from me. He's twenty-eight, a blond, acne-faced air force
fighter pilot from Viet Nam. He was transferred to
Cambodia as an air attaché because he speaks French.
He leaves the air force soon, but during the last five
years he's been a lot of places and bombed—or directed
air strikes onto—a lot of people.

He's a complete hawk, and he believes America
shouldn't "take shit" from any country in the world. He
wants to neutralize China: now, before they get the
bomb. He calls Asians "dinks" and he argues for a
"military solution" to the Viet Nam war.

We talk late into the night: about war, journalism,
democracy, college kids, dissenters, war again and we

disagree on nearly everything. He talks about flying, bringing air strikes in on the "dinks" and getting shot at by the people he is killing. And somehow I'm listening to all this and not getting mad.

Has three months of war reporting dulled my senses that much? He is irrational, racist, brutal and often disgusting. Yet we keep talking.

I feel I'm coming of age as a reporter. I can develop sources without tying myself in knots. But what have I become? I hate everything this man stands for—yet I don't hate *him*. A clergyman would approve, I suppose, but have I become more tolerant—or dulled by the shock of war?

And later, as we weave drunkenly out of the empty house and go separate ways, promising to talk again, I am grateful for a glimpse into this man's boiling, unhappy mind. But I feel bad. Am I beyond rage? What has happened to *my* humanity? I fall asleep in the hotel with the question grinding against my consciousness. But I slip away from it into the night, answering nothing.

The Upside-Down Man

July 9

"This time," I ask the reporter who is driving, "or last time?" He'd been in the town three months earlier.

"Last time," he grunts, pointing to a blackened building, reduced nearly to a pile of bricks.

"That one?" I ask a few seconds later. Ahead, a warehouse's red tile roof had caved in.

"That's new," he says. We are coming into Saang, a small town on a river twenty miles south of Phnom Penh. During the weekend, Communist and Cambodian forces fought in and around the city. Buildings fell and people fled and men died: again.

Last April Saang hosted the first big battle of the new Cambodian war. The town circles a muddy main street and village square on the Bassac River, and that time it was occupied by Communist troops. They withdrew after several days of government bombing and shelling. After they left, the Cambodians continued to shell Saang, nearly destroying it. That was followed by looting.

Saang is also remembered for a sorry bit of psychological warfare. To draw Vietcong fire, one Cambodian general forced Vietnamese refugees to walk into the square carrying a white flag. They were slaughtered. The general later explained that the gunfire revealed Communist positions, making his job easier.

Saang today is a junkyard of bombed buildings, smoking ruins, bricks strewn about, trash and broken glass. I look down at the road and see a black-shirted Vietcong corpse gathering flies, and I stare a moment as the car goes past.

Around a bend, in the center of the market area, I see another man. He swings upside down. The tip of his head, hanging down, is five feet above the street. The rope securing his ankles is tied twenty feet up to a balcony railing. I get out of the car and walk over to him. In doing this, I am aware of my body: breathing, motions inside the chest, heart and lungs, muscles that move as I do or tremble when I stand still, even my eyelids blinking.

His hands are gone, blown off, and his stomach is slashed open and bloody. Naked except for torn shorts leaving his genitals exposed, he twists slowly on the rope. His mutilated arms extend like broken pointers from the charred body as if he is reaching out. He died in an explosion, probably a rocket or grenade. Watching him, I feel myself breathe. The sac of my body expands and contracts as air rushes in and out; life, facing death, asserts itself.

All around him—and me—Cambodian soldiers loot shops and homes. No one stops them. They break into hardware and clothing stores, grocery shops and street stalls, and there are sounds of crunching glass and things being broken. They take shoes, tools, toys—snakeskin drums I hear the soldiers thumping around town now—radios, pastries, anything they can carry away.

Some are robbing stores within the dead man's shadow. The soldiers pass close enough to touch him as they walk in and out of the shops, sometimes grinning at me. I don't return their greetings, and I walk away in anger. The dead man dominates the square. You see him from every angle of it. Wherever I turn he is there: the point of a compass I can't avoid coming back to.

I open some C rations with the other reporters and eat lunch leaning against the car. I look at the canned meat and worry that I won't be able to eat it. I look again at *him*. He swings about fifty yards away. Strangely, the food goes down without trouble. The other reporters eat easily, too. What is wrong with us? Shouldn't we be getting sick, or *something*?

An old Cambodian soldier stops in front of him. "Just like the French," he tells us through a translator. "They always left examples." He says the Cambodians hung three Vietcong bodies. Two were cut down just before we arrived.

While we eat, soldiers burn down a house where some Vietcong spent the night. It is consumed with a loud crackling. Practically every building in Saang is burned or broken. I walk to a shop where a man and his wife are taking a radio and some personal goods out of the rubble. I say hello and they explain that "big guns" were fired into the store last night. I look up at the walls and ceiling. The ceiling is about to fall, and the floor is littered waist-deep with broken furniture and shelf stock.

They nod and bow and show me around as if I were a government inspector. I wish them good luck and, unable to say anything sensible beyond that, excuse myself. I feel dark and disgusted, wanting to spit into the street in a way that will soil the faces of generations of politicians who brought war to Saang and whose armies are destroying Cambodian towns now as if they were cutting down trees. No one remembers the dead except friends and family. Even these memories fade into the darker parts of your mind, gone as a drop of blood evaporating in the street.

One memory, I swear, won't leave me. The meat hanging in the marketplace is a man: a living thing turned into cut-up flesh, exposed mercilessly to the filthy air, his humanity blown away and blackened by fire. A man watching us from behind dead eyes as we ate and continued to live.

As we get into the car I look a last time at him, thinking of symbols men believe in: a cross, a man in a lotus position. There is a tarot card of an upside-down man said to relate a connection between the Divine and the Universe. Somewhere between this storm and the last one in my life, my eye will search to find him again. But I can't know, this day at least, when he will appear.

Analysis of Sorts

July 28
The American soldiers have left, but Cambodia's war
will continue in fits and starts for months, perhaps years.
The argument remains: should Americans have crossed
the border? The editors have scheduled an assessment
of this, but the question is so controversial that they re-
quest separate opinions from each man who covered the
story, knowing these will vary. They hope to weave our
individual mutterings into a broadly scoped analytic
piece. It doesn't work, and the story dies. The following,
edited, is what I filed:

Assessing the move, one is forced to reach for neat
categories, to say it worked or didn't work, that it was
good or it was bad. It *was* a limited military success.
And from the Pentagon's and Saigon's point of view,
that should be enough. But there are larger issues.
America deserved better than another military campaign.
And Cambodia, the pawn, deserves better than its current
economic, political and military disasters.

The military case for intervention was reasonably
sound. In Viet Nam's southern regions the war has now
slowed down. Communist-initiated actions in all but
Viet Nam's northernmost military region have nearly
stopped, in fact, for lack of supplies that once came from
sanctuary areas across the border. Prior to the Cambodian
invasion Communist troops brought tons of supplies in
through Sihanoukville and through landings on the southern Cambodia coast. They also controlled the border
areas and could resupply their people in Viet Nam with
ease.

Now the Sihanoukville route is dead, and last month
U.S. navy ships sank a lone North Vietnamese trawler
off the coast of Kien Hoa Province. American intelligence
has recorded a lot of activity on the Ho Chi Minh trail
lately, a difficult time to transport supplies because of

seasonal rains. The reason, they insist, is that the Communists can now depend only on northern supply routes.

American military spokesmen also argue that eliminating the sanctuary areas is a major tactical victory. The Communists can no longer retreat across the border to safety. Moreover, they've been forced to organize new supply routes through Laos.

This, plus the loss of tons and tons of equipment and rice, have bought "time" for the Allied side. As the American military sees it, the Communists have lost equipment, supply routes, sanctuaries and the capability to wage war in much of Viet Nam. Beyond that, they must spread themselves thin by deploying troops throughout Cambodia.

There are arguments against this, of course. The most important is that "buying time" means nothing. A six-month setback for the Communists only prolongs the war slightly—and its inevitable result. It is also clear that they will adjust to the new military realities. They are building new supply routes quickly. Nothing has changed in Viet Nam's northernmost military region, where they still organize major campaigns. And in the southern three regions it is an open question whether the current decline in military activity so enthusiastically cited by the American army is by necessity—or design.

Directives published long before the Cambodian invasion (COSVN [Vietcong] Resolutions 9 and 14, specifically) order military units in these areas to return to a guerrilla war strategy. Whether or not supply lines and sanctuary areas were lost, major activity should have declined by now. Both resolutions direct soldiers and cadres to organize locally and build political as well as military strength.

It can be argued that this strategy resulted from a lack of military wherewithal. It also is true the Communists think American troop withdrawals will be encouraged by lying low.

It is undeniable, in fact, that Nixon's move hurt the Communists. But it is questionable whether the damage was significant. Tons of equipment, rice, weapons and ammunition were found and destroyed. But much of the material was third-string weaponry: old guns, bullets for nonexistent weapons, antiquated radio gear. Army spokesmen admitted they probably found no more than 50 percent of the Cambodian storehouses. By that logic, the Communists have just as many supplies left. Nixon also boasted that American troops would find COSVN headquarters. It sounded as though he were making a campaign promise. That didn't happen, and the headquarters functions today as smoothly as ever.

Negatively, it is argued that the invasion drove the Communists farther into Cambodia and subjected greater portions of that country to war. Yet the Communists dislike Lon Nol's pro-West regime enough to have advanced into Cambodia anyway. But without an American invasion, they might have settled for Cambodia's northeastern corner and border areas—if Lon Nol had left them alone. That would have left Cambodia in a better position than it is in today.

The future? The Communists organize the countryside, and Lon Nol builds an army while strengthening his frail government. Eventually the two sides will clash definitively. But it is also possible the Communists will need their forces for Viet Nam and cede much of Cambodia back to Lon Nol by default.

For Americans, there are nonmilitary questions. For the first time in this century American students died for demonstrating against war. Domestic frustrations over this war clearly jeopardize the political consensus we must have to function as a nation. For however Viet Nam has divided the nation, the Cambodian invasion has made it worse.

I must conclude with a gut reaction that is more personal than journalistic: whatever the invasion's military value, it only adds to the tragedy in Indochina of twenty years of war. For that reason, beyond logic, I can only view Nixon's decision in negative terms.

Airport Scene

I'm listening to an overweight American with a gold ring on his left pinkie talk to a plump Thai girl in her late twenties. He's educated, maybe forty years old, probably has gone briefly to college—the sort of man you often see in Asia buying trinkets from the street stalls to sell in expensive Fifth Avenue stores. She seems to be his girl friend.

We are sitting on adjacent couches in the Bangkok airport's transit lounge. I'm returning to Phnom Penh after flying in to file a story from our office here. He's headed for Hong Kong, leaving her behind. But they aren't talking about that, or anything in particular. Listen:

". . . this girl, she young, very nice to me, number one. She give me bath, massage, make love. Only 60 baht ($3). Next time I go back, she be wiser, charge more. . . .

"I spend too much money here—$3000 in one month. Girls, gifts, many things. Me cheap Charley with you, but no can help. No have money. I go Hong Kong now, maybe stay three days.

"I no can be sure where I go now. Bangkok nice town, number one. You number one. I come back, see you again. . . ."

Honest. This American is speaking pidgin English. He has a ham-hock arm around this girl. He wears a limp wash-and-wear tropical shirt and huge slacks. He sweats big drops of water like a bloated sponge, especially on the dome of his nearly bald head, and talks in a sing-song broken English as if she were a child.

I admit I've done it, falling into a primitive English with bar girls or taxi drivers. But it depresses me when I do, and it is disgusting to see Westerners do it on purpose. For it shows how racist or at least foolish we can sound in this part of the world. The man assumes the girl understands him better, which might be true. But that doesn't change how demeaning it sounds.

The girl is fat and homely and she seems to take him seriously. She has a silver ring on her left hand. A wedding band? Suddenly they notice I am listening. I'm even taking notes. They are embarrassed and I get up, embarrassed, too, to find another seat. As I walk away, he is still saying "number one" and "cheap Charley" and using the present tense and double negatives.

5

Four months in Asia now, two in Cambodia. A score of reporters are dead or missing on Cambodian highways, and this is not the end of it. I hope I never see those roads again. By comparison, Saigon seems safe, and it is time to rotate back. War reporting, I admit, is exciting. It is compelling to consider questions of life and death. And the risks of reporting the stories add meaning to them. That's the myth of war reporting, anyway. It is impossible not to believe some of it.

But the darkness of what I see drags on me, and I feel a blade cutting into me, going deeper. It will alter the exhilaration to a grayness. As days pass, the mornings will become hotter, the rain at night unending. Dust will cling to my skin even after rain. The women become less soft. The liquor leaves a lasting bitterness, a chalky mouth each morning. Then one day dirty clothes, a dripping shower and lukewarm eggs make it almost impossible to drag into the office, or like anyone when I get there.

Say, Can You See?

Sunset in Saigon. Not a particularly noteworthy time, except when the sky occasionally turns on blue and pink lights. The traffic is bad this time of day, and the air pollution, thanks to the traffic, is worse. I'm in the MACV parking lot, starting the office jeep after a check at the base theater to see what movies are coming.

The military usually assumes its audiences have no brains, so the fare leans heavily toward Westerns, horror movies and Disney flicks. Today is no exception, so I turn into the fading daylight knowing it will be another night at the bars.

Like everything else it standardizes around the world, the U.S. army has a version of sunset. The flag is lowered and loudspeakers play "To the Colors" followed by "The Star Spangled Banner." The rules say that upon hearing these sounds all military men must turn toward the music and salute. They are required to stand at attention until the sound stops.

Few do, of course. Uniformed men everywhere run toward their cars at sunset, hide in doorways or stay inside their offices. The rules say that only people fully outdoors must stand and salute, and it is not fashionable to be caught standing like an idiot and saluting music.

A few men take the ceremony seriously. The music has started now, and one is standing nearby, ramrod-erect with a karate-stiff hand positioned at the precise angle in a perfect salute. Beside him is a tiny Honda, so small that its fat wheels and miniature motor look like a child's mechanized bike. He is potbellied and sweating a little as he stands at attention in the afternoon, wearing a white crash helmet, which, over horn-rimmed spectacles, makes him look like a comedian-astronaut. He is a career sergeant with only four stripes. That means he is a failure: no promotions. The military makes him wear this embarrassment on his arm. A chubby little man on a toy bike with too few stripes. Who could have less dignity?

Perhaps for five achingly long minutes he stands, stiff as a plank, never wavering. I watch, thinking about him, the flag he salutes, the country we both come from. We are alike in many ways, cultural roots, the odd fact that we both make money—for different reasons—off this war. How can he accept a life, humanity hidden behind stripes and metal, which makes him a fool? A toy soldier saluting music.

Now the music has ended, and the sergeant has mounted his Honda and left. I start the jeep again and leave too, concerned with the sunset traffic, pushing him into the recesses of my mind.

A Short One at O'Reilly's

August 28

I'm taking my new bureau chief, a brilliant and sarcastic Harvard graduate named Jon Larsen, through South Viet Nam's northern military areas. He arrived last week to replace Clark, who rotated to Jerusalem. Larsen has dark curly hair, a fiery temperament, and he is barely over thirty. The Vietnamese are stunned to have such a young boss, but Larsen is tough and they can see this.

We are flying over hilly forest canopy country to Firebase O'Reilly, which the North Vietnamese are attacking. Somewhere on New York's West Side, I am thinking, there is a bar named O'Reilly's. The drinkers talk about their troubles and perhaps tell tall tales about previous wars. But here O'Reilly's is a muddy, treeless mountain surrounded by black jungle and more mountains and manned by Vietnamese. The bartender is throwing metal at you, and the drinking is done out of canteens. O'Reilly's in Viet Nam sits astride a Communist supply route to the coast. The Communists need to use it. The exercise goes like this:

A few weeks ago, Vietcong and North Vietnamese troops moved into positions around an American base named Ripcord, nearby and also in the way. Both bases are near the Laotian border. The Communists began with hourly barrages of mortars and rockets at the base. Next, they ambushed infantry units operating outside Ripcord. The Americans called air strikes on them, but it didn't help. The attack got worse and the base had to be evacuated in considerable panic and confusion.

Information officers later said that Ripcord was due to be evacuated anyway, but that was a lie. As men were screaming and dying, helicopters flapped through murderous fire to take people out. One was shot down and it fell into an ammunition dump, blowing up half the base. The confusion was thick. A man lay dead beside the helicopter pad for two weeks of fighting before anybody put him in a chopper. Eventually, blackened, burned, pock-marked Ripcord was empty.

Now the Communists moved toward O'Reilly. Again: mortars, rockets, ambushes. The strategy is to force ground units around the base to retreat to the mountain. No one is left, then, to harass their positions. And if they move carefully, they'll be able to avoid American air strikes. Soon life on O'Reilly mountain, an unhappy dance under a metal thunderstorm, will become so intolerable that it will be time to evacuate.

For now the mountain holds. A North Vietnamese lieutenant defects and reveals the Communist positions. American planes now drop their bombs accurately. Government ground units push out from the base rather than toward it, forcing the Communists to defend themselves. The base has been under fire for three days when Jon and I arrive. Just before landing, the chopper pilot says we have three seconds to get out. We fall over each other jumping off and run for a bunker while he careens off the mountain sideways so the mortar he thinks is coming will miss him.

We have an hour until the helicopter returns. I look out at the hills around us. They have hundreds of tiny parachutes hanging on bushes where flares fell during weeks of night fighting. The white spots look to me like patches of snow. The Vietnamese commander meets us and we go into his bunker for the standard formal briefing complete with charts and graphs. Charts and graphs and maybe a mortar to kill us while we talk.

When the briefing is over, we talk to a young American captain, an "adviser." He shows us where a Vietnamese major leaned against some sandbags the other day, smoking a cigarette. A mortar came in and killed him. The captain is tall and thin, crew cut, and looks like a fellow I knew in a fraternity at Berkeley, but didn't like much. He smiled all the time, so you couldn't tell what he felt about things. The captain is the same way. He says he likes his job, and he is proud to defend this muddy mountain. But he smiles saying this, and I can't tell whether he means it; and so I don't trust him.

The base looks to me like a place to die: barbed wire and gun emplacements where trees ought to be, clay and mud where grass and weeds were stripped away to build shelters. The trees on the mountainside have been defoliated or cut down so sappers can't approach without being seen. A few limbs remain. My mind sees skeletal bones blackened by fire.

Jon and I walk around the flat surface, staring out over the hills. There is nothing to do, no story today. Most of the Vietnamese are huddled in bunkers and small tents, with a GI camped here and there. One sticks his head out of a hole and asks to see the magazine sticking out of my pocket. He glances through it while we wait. We ask how it is up here and he only smiles, saying he hasn't been at O'Reilly long. I expect him to say more. But he doesn't. He wants to stay alive; that's all. And he doesn't want to talk to reporters about it. Bad luck, I suppose.

The helicopter returns and we leave, jumping on like panicked Keystone Cops in the same three-second routine. I'm flustered in the confusion and try to fasten my seat belt as the machine veers off the mountainside, banking sharply to avoid incoming fire. Nobody is shooting, but I grab wildly for a metal post, afraid of falling out. Then, out of range, we straighten out and flap calmly over rice paddies and mountains back to the city of Hue.

Funny. If O'Reilly had been attacked, I am thinking, we might have gotten a good story. But then we might have been killed. You can't have it both ways. My mind is divided about this, but I'm just as glad it worked out the way it did. Larsen can get into trouble without me, I figure, and I suppose he will before his tour is up. But no sense in hurrying things. The fear I felt in Cambodia is shrunk to a mute memory. Nonetheless, I'm hardly a daredevil and I'm unlikely to become one.

On the River

Jon and I are standing on an old wooden plank strung between supporting posts, part of a primitive pier system winding around a community of sampans on Hue's Perfume River. The idea—mine, I ruefully admit—is to rent a boat and sleep tonight on the gently rocking river. This is the last day of our "tour," and I'd read that these little houseboats could be rented overnight, women optional, and the quiet river would lull you into peaceful sleep.

So Jon and I go down to the water, given directions by an ARVN lieutenant, and begin haggling. We've picked a boat and have the deal nearly closed. Then someone mentions girls. I smile without thinking. Suddenly the deal is off. We are directed to a more tawdry boat where a grinning Vietnamese keeps saying "no sweat." He is a wiry little man who moves about his boat in jerky, nervous motions trying to lure us into his keeping. We say we liked the earlier boat. He says this one is "best" for us.

Then it comes. The dock suddenly fills with salesmen. Fishermen bring forward their prepubescent daughters. Toothless hags stand by hopefully. The crowd grows. Children run down the planks to stare at us, giggle and hold out their hands for money. I notice one little boy who stares from another boat. He has very un-Vietnamese blond hair. His belly is puffy from bad food; his nose runs. Except for his stomach and clothing he looks like an American child who would be in a nursery school. Some American has a son and doesn't know it, and his child may die in this waterfront culture, an alien face in an ancestor-worshiping society. We give up and take the boat to get away from all the outstretched hands.

71

As the man poles away, his family takes one end of the sampan, separated from us by a partition. But he won't leave us to join them. He keeps telling stories in broken English and trying to make deals. We are a prestigious catch and he has big plans. Do we want food? A tour of Hue? A young girl? He'll arrange it. He jumps in the river to take a swim in the middle of his sales pitch, climbs back in the boat and vigorously dries himself. We are not impressed.

He finally leaves and we get ready to sleep. No way. The boat is surrounded by other sampans anchored for the night: lamps burning, music, families arguing and talking, clinking dishes as they eat. It is like a New York neighborhood on a hot summer night. The other boats keep banging into us too. Jon gets up cursing and grabs a pole and tries to push us farther out into the river. This brings the little man's wife through the partition in a hurry, making angry noises. She poles us back into place. Then come the mosquitoes. Jon is stretched out on the deck of this floating prison, slapping himself madly. I've bedded down on a mat inside.

I wake up screaming—thinking an animal is crawling on my face. It is a bad dream and Jon laughs loudly. I'm embarrassed and curse him under my breath. Another attempt at sleep. More mosquitoes. Wap-wap-wap! Jon slaps himself and rolls restlessly around. People paddle by to sell Cokes. A woman approaches in a boat and asks for money. Nobody sleeps. I smoke a cigar and we talk, and finally it is morning. Dirty, red-eyed, unshaven, we are poled slowly to land and hand the little man his money. He asks for a tip. We can't believe it. And he is angry when we refuse and he argues.

We turn away and stumble toward the roadway to hitch a ride south. I have this vision of a junior executive taking his boss on a tour of a factory and knocking him into a vat of sludge. Sorry, boss. But I hope you liked the tour otherwise. At least you didn't get killed.

One Future

I am working on a story about Vietcong strength, and An and I are talking about the VC infrastructure or "shadow government." I have heard it is getting stronger, and he agrees. This runs contrary to official pronouncements, and it means the war is not likely to end soon. The Vietcong cadres remain well organized, and tax collection and terrorism continue, directed by cell-linked groups of political and military men who wait for the country's balance of power to change.

It occurs to me, again, that An, a journalist of impeccable reputation, has a lot to lose if North Viet Nam triumphs. He works for Americans, is well known in government and intelligence circles, and disapproves of the Communist way of life.

"Who will win, An?" I ask.

"Oh, the Communists. As soon as the Americans leave."

"What will happen to you?"

"They will not kill me. I am too old. But they will make me work harder. Maybe they will roast my German shepherd [An's favorite pet]. I will no longer be able to sleep as late in the morning. They will make me get up and do exercises in the street. My children will not be able to go to special schools. It will be hard, but we will survive."

He paused. "There is one problem. Many people think I am a CIA agent because I work for an American magazine and went to an American university. If the Vietcong hear this they will shoot me immediately. There will be no time to tell them it isn't true."

"What will you do?"

"I have told my wife not to look for me if an attack comes. I will telephone her. I will be hiding somewhere until it is safe. And if they shoot me—well, I am old, and much of my life is behind me."

An is over forty, old by Vietnamese standards. But he has a young wife and three children to worry about. His biggest problem—having to bend with a government that may break in the future—plagues many Vietnamese. For he is a brilliant and likable man who loves animals and the peace of his neighborhood, one of many quiet streets in Saigon that allow Vietnamese to forget war now and then. But like most Vietnamese he knows the peace cannot last.

The Sporting Life

September 26

I sit today in an oasis of clear water, sweeping trees and well-fed people—in wartime Saigon. This is Le Circle Sportif, a colonialist playground built by the French: a dozen tennis courts, two swimming pools, badminton, Ping-Pong, exercise rooms, restaurants, bars and a stifling atmosphere of decadence.

Add a score of healthy upper-class girls to gaze at, and it naturally follows that I've joined the place. My reasons are no better defended than those of the average Frenchman or draft-exempt Vietnamese. I like tennis, swimming, food and drink, and watching girls. And this is one of the prettiest spots in Saigon—beautifully landscaped and completely devoid of barbed wire.

I should add there is considerable irony to this place. Just driving here, you pass blocks of barbed wire studded with gun emplacements, then jostle with hundreds of poor people on bicycles and Hondas to make a turn out of traffic into the broad driveway.

Then inside, there are constant reminders of Saigon's split personality. I played tennis earlier today with a fellow named Jerry. He's an accountant for one of the American construction firms: tall, thin, crew cut with a hazy, untroubled look behind watery blue eyes. Afterward we sat in the courtside bar drinking iced tea and watching people in starched white costumes bat balls back and forth.

I asked how long he'd been in Saigon.

"Four years."

I whistled softly in surprise. Four years in Saigon?

Jerry looked at me as if I lacked good manners.

"It's not bad at all," he said testily. "Saigon is really

75

just like any other city. You can live here without even noticing the war."

I had this flash of Jerry talking to country-club friends in the suburbs in a few years: ". . . Viet Nam? We belonged to a nice club. Good tennis, swimming, nice people, you know? Servant problems occasionally. And once in a while the government causes trouble—theirs, not ours. And it got a bit depressing with all the soldiers and barbed wire around. But after a while, we didn't notice. I kept in good shape—played a lot of tennis, even took scuba lessons by the pool. . . ."

Beyond the tennis courts are the swimming pools, filled with rich kids happily splashing about and ringed by bikini-clad French and Asian girls. The girls are delicious: tall, thin, dark and often pouty lipped, with black hair sometimes falling in long waves as far as their tiny waists.

At noon today the poolside is cluttered with journalists and American embassy people. Teen-agers play tag, pushing each other in the pool, and matrons in tank suits spread tanning lotion on their flabby backs. A nice place to relax—but I am often drawn to the patio railing. It is a startling place to observe the contrast between rich and poor.

Le Circle's land borders the national palace, and between the club and the palace is a no-man's-land of bunkers and military emplacements for troops in the palace guard. Directly below the pool—you could jump there from the patio railing—are the homes and families of the soldiers: tin and wood single-room huts with naked children playing outside in mud, trash and barbed wire.

ARVN soldiers are paid so little that it is hardly worth listing their salaries—between $12 and $20 a month for a man with a wife and three kids. The shantytown below looks like most peasant communities in Asia. A toddler with a runny nose squats near a pile of trash, picking up bottle caps and pieces of metal. A woman washes clothes in a big metal pot. Three soldiers are drinking beer at a table in front of one of the shacks. And barbed wire, of course, is all around.

I'm watching this scene from about thirty feet away. As the kid toddles toward a trash pile nearer the barbed wire, I turn from the railing and walk back to the pool, glancing at a shapely Vietnamese teen-ager with a peace sign hanging on a chain above breasts barely covered by her bikini top.

The water is cool and the sun, as usual at this time of day in Saigon, burns hard on my back. A few months ago the Vietcong shot some rockets into town and one landed in a tennis court, blowing it up. It is fixed now, but I bet the soldiers are looking forward to the next volley; and the sooner the better.

Trinh Phu

We are looking down Rach Vop Canal. It is raining and the canal is muddy, and it is stirred by the wind into rows of small waves. There are trees on both sides of the water, and rice fields behind them stretch as far as I can see.

Joe McBride, a Pacification worker who believes in what he does and is fat from twelve months of army chow, points toward a skinny boat sitting low in the water. It rocks uneasily as we climb in, settling lower. We motor down the waterway, past an old temple as I sit cross-legged watching the shoreline, to a small market-place where I see some Vietnamese officials waiting.

Joe is an untenured foreign-service officer. He wears glasses, has a pimply complexion and bulges in the middle like a ripe pear. I like him. He is young, honest, open, brave, enthusiastic—real Americana. In fact, so much of it that sometimes I stand back and look at him in amazement. This is his first assignment for the State Department. He works hard, and he is doggedly honest. He already has a bad name at the province Pacification headquarters for resisting the wrongdoing he sees around him: the American officials who falsify reports, the Vietnamese district chief who steals public-works money.

Yet I think that Joe doesn't connect the larger and smaller problems of his involvement here (the district chief is corrupted because American money is *there*, etc.) as do many of our generation. He believes in American foreign policy, at least his role in it, and he will spend at least eighteen months of his life, his tour of duty, in risk and discomfort, trying to make it work. After all of America's unhappiness over Viet Nam, his dedication is hard for me to understand.

The word *pacification* is part of the official language

of Viet Nam. The term is so common that it is seldom defined. As a result I don't really know what it means—even after six months here. To remedy this I picked a hamlet in the Delta, part of Joe's district as it happened, which had in the last year come under government control. That is, it had been "pacified." This one, named Trinh Phu, now has a "D" rating. That means government control is shaky. But a year ago it was "V"—Vietcong controlled.

A little government control means "E." A little more gives the hamlet a "D." And so on up the line to "A," which is said to be full government control. The rating system (Hamlet Evaluation System or HES) is seldom accurate, however, for it is based on evaluations by foreign service or military men whose careers depend on their district's improving. Most districts are about one grade above what they should be.

We get out of the boat and I shake hands with half a dozen Vietnamese: soldiers, Rural Development cadres, local government officials. Then Joe introduces me to Tran Van Giao, a bony farmer with skin coarse and brown from working outdoors all his life. He wears oversize rubber boots and a black rain slicker and he is the hamlet chief. He owned land in Trinh Phu during the fifties, Joe says. Then the Vietcong took over, and during a land-reform program made him part with six of his eleven acres of rice fields. Angry and frightened, he moved to a neighboring area controlled by the government. When government forces finally returned to Trinh Phu last year, he moved back and was made hamlet chief until elections were held. Then he was elected.

My coming has caused a commotion, and scores of townspeople are out to watch, crowding around. The day has been arranged carefully. The Vietnamese district leader has sent a hand-picked ARVN captain as guide and interpreter, and we are surrounded by pistol-packing black-shirted Rural Development cadres. I ask to talk to Tran, so we walk to a lookout post behind the market area. The chief squats as he talks and he avoids my eyes.

He says his security is "fair." Someday he hopes to have "a place for women to have babies" in the hamlet. He also wants electricity.

I glance at the rice fields and clusters of trees to the north. These are controlled by the Vietcong. The ARVN officer translates as Tran talks, but Joe has an interpreter, too. Joe says afterward the captain omitted the hamlet chief's most critical comments. Sometimes Tran starts a line of thought unfavorable to the government and the captain nods and frowns. Tran stops.

Trinh Phu had been controlled by antigovernment forces almost without interruption since World War II, Joe tells me. The Viet Minh left after the Geneva settlements in 1954, but Communist cadres stayed behind clandestinely and began to emerge in positions of power by 1957. The hamlet's land is divided by the canal. During the brief years of government control it was safe to travel and fish there. But by 1958 the Vietcong had gained control of a large land area around and including the canal.

It was then booby-trapped. The Saigon government in turn declared the Trinh Phu area a free-fire zone. By such rules, anyone who lived there could be shot as a Vietcong. To avoid this, many families moved out to remote areas or over to government-controlled districts. The marketplace fell silent, and there seemed to be little life in Trinh Phu.

Government forces moved through the area occasionally, Joe adds, but they never stayed, and the Vietcong weren't seriously challenged. On Pacification maps, the area was an embarrassing blotch of red V's. That was fixed a few years ago. The Saigon government gerrymandered seven hamlets into one and called it "Trinh Phu." The result was six fewer V's, though nothing had changed. Tran, in fact, still thinks his hamlet is one-seventh as big as the government says.

Joe and I leave the lookout post. I want to motor down the canal and see other parts of Trinh Phu. The district chief had told me flatly yesterday the canal was "secure."

He is an ARVN major and his soldiers built a school-house for Trinh Phu last spring without metal supports for the concrete columns in order to pocket the leftover public-works money. I could travel Rach Vop safely, he said.

But today the ARVN captain says no boats are available. He suggests a walk. Joe says the captain figures I will get tired and want to go home. I plan to surprise him. We follow a path along half a mile of muddy bank, sliced up by canal inlets which have to be crossed on shaky bamboo logs. It is a difficult trip, and after an hour I insist again on the boat ride. Joe backs me up, so the captain finds one. It is raining harder now and there is no sun. Water slops around in the bottom of the boat as I climb in. A Vietnamese motorman, wet and shaking from the chilly afternoon, pushes us through the muddy waves. ARVN soldiers are stationed behind banana trees, in case the area isn't as secure as the district chief says. I hear single shots ahead signaling that the area is clear. Tension creeps into the small of my back. I feel stiff and I flinch sometimes when the shots are fired.

The canal was first "cleared" when soldiers came through Trinh Phu last year and built two triangular outposts on the canal about two miles down from the market. The Communists attacked immediately and they were driven back. That established the government's presence. Officially, the hamlet was rated "E." Terrorism and minor fighting followed. Government cadres came in and built more outposts and a thatched-roof school. Because they had military protection, fishermen used the canal again and the marketplace became active. Eventually Trinh Phu was rated "D." That means "marginal security" and "regular covert activity" by the Vietcong.

I huddle cross-legged again on the floor of the boat, soaked even though I wear a poncho. Rain is dripping off my hat brim onto my face, and I'm sitting in several inches of water. I feel something special about this ride. After a few minutes, it suddenly seems frozen in time

81

and space. I look at my watch. Raindrops are bouncing off its crystal hypnotically. Beneath the glass the watch says 3:30 P.M. The day is gray. The water is brown, and moving fast. I feel the war is very near. Along the canal bank I see broken trees and burned fields now, signs of recent fighting. I feel caught in the current as we sweep downstream, my eye perceiving a confluence of rain, wind and violence, and I know if something happens now, there is nothing I can do.

A pause in time. I am drifting as if falling like sand through the eye of an hourglass.

Someone waves to an outpost ahead. I shake myself as we pull up to shore and get out. It is filled with young soldiers, their wives and babies. They smile a lot and crowd around, astonished that so many VIPs, including a *bao chi* ("newsman") would visit in such poor weather.

We talk and I take pictures. Then I ask to go farther down the canal. The captain says it is too late in the day. Joe and I say we'll risk it, bluffing. The captain scowls. Then he admits the canal isn't secure beyond here.

We ride back to the market. It is getting late. The boat passes the district chief's new school, which is already falling down, then a rice mill with a yellow government flag outside. Joe turns to me and says the owner pays "insurance" to the Vietcong. It is nearly dark and we still have to drive back to district headquarters. I watch Joe on the way home. He is a good man, honest and intelligent. How will he feel about this job twenty years from now? I settle back in the Land Rover's front seat, tired and wet, but I don't ask the question out loud.

Bombs Away

We are flying. The air is filled with tiny clouds stretching like cotton beads toward the horizon. Below there are forests and rice paddies, and sometimes the paddy water flashes with the sun's reflection.

I am writing a story on the Vietnamese air force, riding today with one of its pilots. I've long wanted to fly in a fighter—boyish notions of swashbuckling, I admit—but now that it is happening I am paralyzed, locked into a rigid mind-fix focusing only on the passing moment. For something in me refuses to accept the larger fact of being here: flying north, voluntarily trapped in the copilot's seat of an ancient Vietnamese bomber, about to drop four thousand pounds of explosives on people I've never met.

As the fighter churns through the bright morning air, shaking, held aloft by a single propeller, I am continually aware of an odd separation of mind and body. Back at the air base my mind turned away from me, pretending the trip was a rich joke, asking in laughing tones if I would really get *in* this mottled gray machine. Then I climbed in, mind still questioning body, yet each of them aware the questions had no meaning. My future and this plane had merged.

Once in the plane, my mind refuses to function. Mechanically I strap myself into the seat and hook up the parachute mechanism. Then I locate the ejection lever (a yellow rope between my legs)—plug in my radio headset and tighten the chin strap on my white Captain Midnight–style helmet.

The man in the driver's seat is Captain Hoang Manh Dzung, an easygoing Vietnamese airman with a broad toothy grin and thick black hair. He's twenty-eight, has

83

a wife and a child, and his bland features and rectangular, smooth face suggest he ought to live in a suburb and sell insurance. I sit beside him, zombilike, outwardly calm and interested as he explains how to work the ejection rope and the radio. He cranks up the engine, which sounds like a buzz saw breaking glass.

We taxi onto the runway. Captain Dzung revs up the engine to test it and talks to the control tower. Then he closes the canopy, separating us from the outside world. Somehow I didn't believe we were going until this moment. I lean back and keep saying, ". . . there's nothing you can do now, nothing you can do . . ."

After we level off, the other half of today's team, another skyraider, approaches on the right wing. He flies alongside for a few crazy moments while I wonder if he'll misjudge the distance and crash into us. Then he waves and peels off, Hollywood style.

We are moving toward the Cambodian border when someone on the radio diverts us to Lai Khe, a Vietnamese infantry headquarters about thirty miles north of Saigon. As we approach, I see the base several miles off the right wing. Below is our target area, a small forest bounded on two sides by canals and a gully on the third. A small wooden bridge stretches across the ravine. Apparently we are going to drop our thunder—sixteen five-hundred-pound bombs between the two ships—into the tree line just left of the bridge. From this height the landscape looks liks bumps on a topographic map.

"The target today," a cordial voice on the earphones informs us, "is a suspected enemy location near the gully behind that clump of trees. I'll try to point it out as we go by."

The voice sounds like someone on the telephone, and comes from a silver speck several thousand feet below, a spotter plane with an American pilot inside who is darting about and feeding us information as he sizes up the target. Apparently he spotted this "suspected" Vietcong area and called for an air strike just as we were passing by.

"Surface winds are calm," he continues. "Negative report on ground fire [I stop breathing so hard]. I'd like you to make your first run north to southwest."

Numbers and coordinates are given followed by mutual OKs between the American, who is called a "Forward Air Controller," and Captain Dzung. Silence while the American checks with ground control, then he calls our radio sign.

"OK, Phoenix Khaki, do you read me?" Captain Dzung's squadron is nicknamed Phoenix, and the call signs each day are coordinated by color.

"Roger-reayou-loun-clear," returns the captain in slurred, minimal English.

"I want you to drop your first ordnance right at the beginning of the tree line," the voice continues.

By now, we are circling over the forest. I can't see a thing except treetops. The canals and the ravine with the bridge over it are off to one side.

We are banking heavily on our left wing, tilting at nearly ninety degrees. I keep reaching for something to grab. A subway strap? Safety handles? The plane is old, built in 1954. It is a noisy beast, a clanking jalopy in the sky, particularly terrifying now that we are riding sideways.

Suddenly Captain Dzung stands the plane on its nose and dives. The ground looms up like a 3-D movie, seen first through the canopy top upside-down. Now we are above the jungle and I see—I think I see—a brown, tube-shaped bomb drop from the right wing. In that same instant the g-force falls like an avalanche as we pull out of the dive. My head and shoulders are shoved toward the floor, hard. All I can see is Captain Dzung pulling the stick fiercely toward him.

As we climb out, the FAC comes on the earphones again.

"Very nice, number one," he says, pep talking like a football coach. "Very nice hit. You're right on the button."

Our plane is "number one" and the sister ship is "number two." The other pilot follows our run, instructed to bomb "one-zero meters to the left," and I can see smoke and fire coming out of the trees.

We repeat this routine seven times while the forest explodes. The FAC is our cheerleader: "right on the money, number one! Move one-zero to the right now. Very nice, very nice. Now try to hit ten meters short of number two's hit in the trees please. Nice, nice!"

Finally, thank God, it is over. We circle the jungle while the FAC flies down to inspect the damage. "One hundred percent of the bombs were on target," he radios. "Negative secondary explosions"—meaning we didn't hit any ammunition caches. And possibly meaning there was no one down there in the first place.

That happens a lot: the pilot flies his mission at thousands of dollars an hour, considerable risk to himself, and drops his bombs on trees. That's better, I suppose, than killing people—but let's not get into that. I feel contaminated enough just being here.

The bombing report is followed by some technical information, then the sign-off: "Thank you and see you next time."

"Roger and thank you," repeats Captain Dzung, bland and businesslike. We fly back to the air base, and I am thinking all we have to do is get this machine on the ground and I am safe. Finally we touch ground and I never felt better in my life.

I tell all the other pilots who crowd around, yes, thank you, I had a good flight and I feel fine. The pilots are folksy warriors who lounge around the squad room, pistols hanging low. One fellow plays a guitar. Others are playing cards, leaning against lockers or reading newspapers. Once I wanted to be like them. Now I want to scream that I don't approve of war, that killing is senseless and nothing about flying or bombing is glamorous or awe inspiring.

But all I do is smile and shake hands and know that I will tell the story of my bombing run again and again, laughing and looking brave as I do it, protesting each time about the immorality of war.

More Bombs

October 15

Another bombing run. My story requires flying in VNAF's oldest and newest planes, so today I try a needle-nosed F-5 Freedom Fighter. This is a cheap, short-range supersonic hot rod which America makes and sells to countries wanting a low cost but shiny jet fighter-bomber force. The Vietnamese are proud of it and want to show it off to me.

There are three planes today, totaling six thousand pounds of bombs. I'm wearing a pressure suit and oxygen mask, and the plane itself is more complicated than yesterday. I can't figure out how to work the ejection mechanism though it is explained twice.

As we take off, the oxygen mask claws at my face, and I am worried about blacking out at the high speeds. A switch near my right hand clicks back and forth between regular air and pure oxygen. Mostly, I use oxygen, but I feel guilty (am I using up the supply?) and periodically switch to regular air. Today I am behind the pilot. The ride is smoother—and faster—450 mph.

We fly to Cambodia, deep into it. I have a camera and earlier had asked to photograph the other two planes. It is an amazing scene; they are *performing* for me. They pull overhead and fly in a wing-tip formation and wait while I snap them. Then to the left, one over the other. Should I try the right side? How about a close-up? My pilot gives directions over the radio and these metal monsters dance like playful porpoises up and down, back and forth. OK, I'm finished. Now let's drop the bombs.

A few minutes later, we circle a large jungle and rubber plantation area near Kompong Cham. The FAC says all the same enthusiastic things as we dive toward the trees at speeds up to 550 mph. This time the g-force

87

is softened by the pressure suit, which inflates with a pop as we pull out of each dive.

The FAC says the bombs are on target again.

We fly swiftly and uneventfully back to the air base. I think all the way about how the plane will land and I will get out and touch ground and never do this again. The jet is a beautiful, exciting machine, and I freely admit, as I said yesterday, that I've fantasized for years about flying in one.

But now that's taken care of, and I'm turning in my fighter-pilot wings. Let them continue the war without me. Please.

6

In New York now, the leaves are turning gold. It is time to wear a leather jacket, pour coffee and drink it deep like you couldn't in summertime. Smell the wind, walk in Central Park crunching leaves under your boots, buy a bag of hot chestnuts. . . .

Enough. Today and tomorrow are Saigon. The rattling Hondas which crowd and dirty the streets, the rank street stands, the rain and heat, the guns and flares popping at night to remind you someone is dying, again. I awoke this day feeling very, very alone. Loneliness with leaves blowing at your feet and fingers of cold creeping through your jacket was bearable. But here the unmoving air closes around me and there is no way to escape the sadness I feel.

I remember a wind last spring in Cambodia, whipping across the tops of banana trees and promising rain and thunder just before a battle on Route One. I liked it a little, for it drove the fear from my gut into my head where it collided with my imagination. It caused a flushed excitement that makes life, at times, almost good. Saigon needs a few windy days like that.

Raindrops

Four days of rain, and I'm trying to reach Chu Lai, head-quarters of the Americal division, on an important job. It is pouring like hell as we taxi down the Saigon run-way, so hard that we stop and sit on the tarmac, engines buzzing like we are going somewhere, for nearly two hours. I am practically deaf when the C-130 cargo ship is finally cleared and we lift off into the storm.

Chu Lai is the second leg of this bumpy milk run. But already, after an hour's flight, the plane is in trouble. We can't land at the first stop, An Khe, because of the storm: two passes, down, down . . . down—and suddenly up, leaving my stomach behind. For me, the tension of long, blind descents—no window to look out of—is unbearable. It is true for others, too. People begin reaching for the "barf bags" on the walls, and soon the plane is a ghostly collection of pale, half-masked faces. A Vietnamese cor-poral spills his stomach into one bag, peering over the top with fearful eyes. An American lieutenant across the aisle meticulously takes a folded plastic bag from his briefcase and leans into it. The job of pushing his innards up and out brings tears. He wipes his eyes with a hand-kerchief, then cleans his glasses. I stand up, walk a little, and think about fresh air and green fields, hoping I won't throw up. Finally the plane levels off.

Trying to land at Chu Lai is worse. We make three passes, only to be waved away at the last moment. Every-one in the plane is sick or close to it. There isn't an un-used barf bag left. On the third time down, the plane seems to me to be turning upside down, lost from orbit and tumbling toward an eternity of more tumbling and darkness. We fall and fall . . . and finally straighten out and head for Da Nang, the biggest city in northern South Viet Nam. I begin to wonder what will happen if we can't land there.

The reason for this trip is that Lt. William Calley, on trial for atrocities at My Lai, has returned to South Viet Nam. He is looking for evidence to support his side of the story. He arrived in Saigon yesterday, heavier than I remembered when I covered his pretrial hearings at Fort Benning nine months ago. He refused to talk to reporters, barely smiling as he got off the plane. He must hate us. For a year we've hounded him about killing children, his ethics, morality, manhood. Now he is returning to Americal division headquarters—his parent command when My Lai happened—and the army refuses to let us watch. Will he visit My Lai itself? It will be an important story if he does.

We land at Da Nang in a downpour. To everyone's relief, there is no trouble: a normal approach and a routine landing in the rain. But Chu Lai is still forty miles away and I can't get there because of the rain. All roads leading to it are under water. I call the Da Nang press center to get a bunk for the night. The weather report says the flood will be here by evening.

I am edgy five minutes after reaching the press center, a cluster of buildings on a river with a dining hall. Without Calley, I have no story to write. I've seen the movie that's playing; the people at the bar are boring. And it hasn't stopped raining all day. I hear on the radio that two UPI people, Frank Frosch and Kyoichi Sawada, are dead in Cambodia. They were dragged from a car on a road south of Phnom Penh and executed by North Vietnamese. Someone suggests a farewell drink. It is set for 10:00 p.m., but nothing happens. Everyone drinks silently, and I think how awful journalism can be. If you get killed, you can probably count on a nice obituary. But your friends will be writing *other* stories before you are buried, and no one will talk, after a while, about why you died or what it meant.

Daybreak. It is raining again. A Vietnamese reporter for UPI has a friend in the Da Nang police department. Somehow he gets a jeep, complete with driver. I get into the wet and muddy machine, happy to be accomplishing *something*, and it weaves around bunches of peasants walking beside the road in the rain as we head south. Twenty minutes later, the highway disappears into flood waters. The driver stops and talks to a policeman about road conditions. It is apparent we aren't going anywhere. A few Vietnamese on motorbikes plunge ahead, only to be stopped by gun-wielding MPs.

Other Vietnamese, stranded for now, are making the most of the flood. I watch the soldiers tossing beer cans into the flood waters to shoot at them. The noise sounds like fighting—kapow! pow! splash! Our driver gets out, takes his carbine and joins the crowd. He leans on the jeep's hood and makes geysers and waves around an empty Schlitz can in the muddy water.

Behind us, some kids chase a fat, angry sow escaped from her pen. They hold her tail, grab at her legs. She squeals and snarls and pulls them along, trying to bite the ones who come too close. A wagon rolls by with a dead water buffalo in back (drowned? shot?), and I sit in the jeep reading a crumpled paperback novel about a black American writer in Paris who is killed by the CIA and peering out the foggy windows at all this. The peasants standing around in pointed conical hats look to me strangely like clothespins crowded together. The water on the road is said to be ten feet deep in some places.

Dinner at the press center is a dull, defeated thing. A few reporters drag in from Chu Lai, having flown there before the weather got bad. To get to Da Nang, they drove and walked through water that was sometimes armpit deep. One group lost a car in the floods and they had to be rescued by helicopters. Everyone is wet, tired, and getting colds or flu. I didn't miss anything. No one could see Calley anyway and the rain was even worse there. One AP reporter got "arrested" by the army for venturing too close to Calley's trailer. A photographer waited six hours in the storm outside the trailer. Calley finally came out but the pictures were poor because of the rain. Everyone is complaining of jammed cameras and wondering aloud what it will cost to repair them.

Worse yet, the kitchen is flooded and the Vietnamese staff has gone home. No hot food. Cheese sandwiches and coffee, and the water is creeping into the dining room. Even the bar is closed, a foot of water behind it. Outside, rats are running into camp to escape the swollen river. GIs are killing them with ax handles and warning people about snakes. The center's boat was swept away hours ago; the dock went around dinnertime. All the guest sleeping quarters, built at ground level like motel rooms, are flooded. In some, the water is higher than the beds. Our situation is so bad that I feel like laughing.

But soon the mood changes. Nearly everyone is glad to be out of Chu Lai. Few of the reporters just arrived have eaten today, and cheese sandwiches are better than nothing. A lieutenant wearing rubber boots reopens the bar. He pulls out canned peanuts, and we all slosh over to get wet inside, too. *Star Trek* is on TV and everyone has stories to tell. People splash in and out of the bar, moving mattresses into the dining room, balancing them on tabletops. I drink coffee liquor over ice and talk to the wife of a wire reporter. She is young and attractive, and the conversation is pleasant. At 10:30 P.M., according to army regulations, the bar closes. We move into the flooded dining room, taking several bottles of Scotch.

A marine officer inexplicably arrives with a huge double-layer cake, dry. One reporter has a tape recorder and a cassette of Simon and Garfunkel's hit, "Bridge over Troubled Waters." Cigars are passed out and we are soon awash in Scotch and bad jokes about floods. The gathering breaks up at midnight. We slop out into the downpour and navigate through thigh-deep water to our beds.

The Street Kid

I don't know his name. He is tough, skinny, curly-haired and dark, and tall for an Asian kid. Unlike most who hustle spare change, he has a wide smile and you give him money because you like him, not because he is persistent, horribly deformed or a nuisance. His flat nose and slightly Afro hair suggest he has black blood. But he has been alive longer than American GIs have been in Viet Nam, and you can only speculate who came here before that. He is barefoot and wears only ragged dirty shorts, and I don't know how to help him. I'm not sure, in fact, he wants anything I can give.

I can't remember when I first noticed him. Probably parking the jeep one day, because he and other street kids sleep in the open cars. You find them playing inside, asleep on the seat, or just sitting having some place to be. Most move out quietly, sometimes sullenly, but this one smiles at you, laughs, and stands in the street directing you out of the parking spot with utmost seriousness, skinny arms flailing and fingers pointing.

He also directs people into parking spaces. Occasionally I see him washing a car. I am one of his regular benefactors and he whistles or yells a greeting from the curb as I drive by, follows me to the car when I leave the hotel, greets the car as I drive up. I give him money in small amounts and inquire about his well being in the few words we can exchange. He always smiles and nods brightly during each encounter. I imagine his IQ would be high if it were tested.

A few months ago, I made a serious effort to do something other than drop piasters in his pocket. A friend named Dick Hughes, an ex-actor from New York, runs several homes for street kids. He raises the money and lets

95

the kids live as freely as possible. So I put him in my jeep and went to one of the homes, a noisy corner building near a railroad station.

He was shy at first, cowed and silent, but the Vietnamese students who work as counselors there talked to him and said he could stay. He seemed willing. I went back to see him every few days for a couple of weeks. Dick said he was adjusting well, so well and so soon that it was remarkable.

But shortly after that he was on the streets again. I couldn't understand why and asked him through a translator. He said the house had too many rules. The students confirmed this. He was well behaved but he didn't like having to come in at night, one of Dick's few solid rules. They said I should give him money "if you love him," and that he'd come back to the house if he needed or wanted to. Other than that, leave him alone.

I didn't know what to do. It is hardly an accomplishment to give a kid spare change, smile and shake hands, and talk like an older brother. He'd rejected full-time help. Now he was in the streets again, cold and wet, and I couldn't do anything. But he was also free, a friend pointed out, and that probably meant more than anything else.

I was still troubled. No one can live in the streets for long. You get sick, and sooner or later you get in trouble with the law. So one day I asked him what he thought would happen when he got older. And without pausing he raised his hands to aim an invisible M-16, pumping a burst of imagined bullets into the building across the street. He was excited by the idea. He would be infantry, and the thought made him grin.

I was sickened at the idea. But it occurred to me that a place to belong, even the army, was more than he had now. He would eat regularly and get paid, and maybe find a wife and—if he lived—raise kids. Maybe he would run away again. But then you can hope he'll fool all of us and live to see a dozen grandchildren, none of whom will be asking the Americans for handouts.

Boredom and
(a Little) Madness

November 29

It has been goddamn dull lately. The magazine has no space to spare and stories are backed up around the globe waiting for what little is available. And if they have the space, the editors lately have been screwing up what they *take*. I took a beating recently on one story I liked a lot. In little ways, the New York people castrated it: send them a raging bull and it returns a calf. A few weeks ago I got into an argument with them over another story and stupidly lost my temper. Result: I got my knuckles rapped—several times, in successive cables, even after it was over and no rage remained as a defense against being told I was wrong.

Today I feel low and I am getting sick of Saigon. I'm tired of endless war talk with the same people, bad movies, poker, too many nights at Mimi's Bar. The war gets more depressing each day. Add bad traffic, air pollution, stupid press conferences, petty office politics, hustlers and beggars on the streets. I'm getting stoned more and liking it more. I have colds and flu constantly from the food or the air conditioning or the dampness at night. There is no one to talk to, and I think of home a lot: San Francisco, New York, coffee houses, theater, talking about something besides war, hot bagels, live folk music, American women, restaurants, good movies.

The holiday season is here. I had Thanksgiving dinner with a few friends—and between the turkey, cranberry sauce and conversation, it was nice, sort of.

But Christmas . . . Christmas! . . . It's not even December and I feel the season coming like an overcast day. My folks sent me a Christmas package. I taped a holiday

97

message to them last Sunday and nearly started sniffling in the middle of it.

I hear you can get trees from Dalat. Lights and tinsel are already selling on the black market. At the PX the other day, I heard a schmaltzy Perry Como recording of "Home for the Holidays." And I began to get depressed. This is my first Christmas outside America; no stories and a lonely tropical holiday coming. It looks bad.

Folly at Five O'Clock

December 5

Ordinarily, I avoid the so-called "five o'clock follies" unless something big is happening. I don't need the daily statistics of death and bombs dropped, delivered in one-dimensional dullness by MACV's gray spokesmen, for most of the stories I do.

The briefing is always unpleasant. It is hot and crowded, and there is little *really* factual information. We figured out once that if "allied" forces had killed everyone listed on the tabulation sheets over the years the North Vietnamese army would have been fully exterminated—several times. This is not a war of body counts anyway. But nobody has told MACV, so the follies—which actually start at 4:15 P.M.—go on day after day flirting with statistical absurdity.

This is a sillier week than most. The Green Berets raided a North Vietnamese prison camp at Son Tay the other day. They did the job well, dropping in below the radar net, surprising everyone. Unfortunately, there were no American prisoners there. Bad ending.

The raid was secret, but now, because Hanoi announced it over the radio, the Pentagon admits several days after the fact: yes, it did stage a raid. We go to the follies thinking we'll get additional information so the story, which happened in Southeast Asia, doesn't come entirely from Washington.

But the MACV briefer only reads excerpts from the Washington press conference. He says he has nothing to add. We are angry as hell. One reporter is so upset he vomits afterward. I turn to an air force colonel who is the most honest military mouth I know. He says he is "embarrassed," but he can't talk. This happens often.

News from this part of the world is released first, sometimes exclusively, in Washington. It is maddening!

For several days, the MACV briefers read us more excerpts from Washington press conferences. We scratch around town desperately for sources. I pick up a few things but it is obvious that few people in Saigon knew about the raid in advance. Perhaps only Bunker and Abrams. The town has never been so tight, and our relations with MACV's press people get worse each day.

A Spy Story

There's a restaurant on Nguyen Hue Street named Valenco's: small, old-world French, deep brown and red colors, good food and a thick atmosphere that reminds you of Bogart and old spy movies. It has a graying Corsican proprietor, a voluptuous hostess named Jacqueline and a small bar up front.

I eat there occasionally. The food is good, and I know Jacqueline. I dated a friend of hers briefly and she dated a friend of mine. During dinner, she comes to my table and we talk until my French breaks down. Now she's seeing another friend: a fierce, slightly crazy CIA agent who is also crafty, smart and likable. He keeps a loaded .45 in his briefcase and sees shadows everywhere. And he sometimes shares information with me. It never fails to check out.

Mark—not his real name—is young, lean and good looking, and he sees Jacqueline regularly. He says he hasn't slept with her, which may be true. But they are playing a strange game. Jacqueline is an exotic, sensual girl: French-Cambodian, wide smile, powerful body, dark hair. I assume she is beyond parlor games.

Mark and I sit at the bar tonight, waiting for her to get off work so we can go to a party. He is in one of his more spooky moods—glowing eyes, heavy, heavy talk of conspiracy and death—when a bespectacled crew-cut man walks in and sits down at a stool near us.

"Cool it," Mark intones, and nods to the man, who nods back.

We talk idly for a moment—it isn't good for Mark to be seen with a reporter—then something trips inside him and he starts talking in low, hushed tones. Here's the story:

Jacqueline, he says, is an agent for Le Deuxième

Bureau, the French CIA. She has worked for the Viet-cong, which in turn has dealings with Le Bureau. Jacqueline's employer, the graying Corsican, bosses LDB in Saigon. And Valenco's, along with his other restaurant, La Casita, is a hangout for French, American, even Italian spooks.

Jacqueline slept with my other friend, who gets publicity occasionally, because it was thought he worked for the American government. Jacqueline and Mark met on a rainy night months ago in Saigon. She ran up to his car, pursued by armed Vietnamese soldiers. Mark didn't know her, but he opened the car door and they sped away and have been seeing each other since.

Now they are acting out a classic spy drama: flirtation and trickery, each waiting. Mark is convinced that Jacqueline, though she uses only Vietnamese, Khmer and French in public, speaks flawless English. Jacqueline's job is simply to circulate and pass on information. He says she is an experienced "fifth columnist."

I sip Pernod and wonder how much of this to believe. Mark's mind works in strange ways and I sometimes suspect that in it fantasy and reality have adjoining bedrooms. Yet we are friends, an alliance formed through hundreds of conversations, and I've concluded that Mark is no more crazy than his environment—the half-lit maze of corridors that intelligence people must wander in. I'm inclined to believe much of what he tells me—perhaps minus some Hollywood touches.

The crew-cut man with glasses doesn't figure in the story, except he happens to be a CIA gunman. He is a hired assassin. Mark trained with him once. They made nighttime forays through a swamp loaded with electronically controlled traps. The exercise was to shoot the dummy gunman before he shot you. Mark says the man never missed.

I am absorbing this with wide-eyed fascination. Should I laugh? Believe him? Mark concludes, smiling savagely: "If you write about this, you might get killed."

I say I have no intention of doing a story, and then I

remember something else. I spend a lot of time with Mark in bars and around the Circle Sportif pool, dealing with him both as a friend and as a source. If Jacqueline and Mark watch each other, and the crew-cut man drinks in Valenco's and the French proprietor sees me with Mark and Jacqueline regularly, then I, too, am watched. . . .

We leave Valenco's and go to a party on the outskirts of town. The villa is big and roomy, the women are fascinating and the liquor is good. I am thinking about spies as I dance with a petite Vietnamese girl named Evette who works as a translator at the American embassy. Of course she's not a spy, but tonight I am not so sure.

On Being a Westerner

Nha Be is a small district of rice fields and villages about twenty miles from Saigon. The American "adviser" there is Hank Bassford, and I've made an appointment to talk with him about the Pacification program.

At the office, Dang draws a map which gets me to the district, but he doesn't know where the CORDS (Pacification) office is. The day is hot and I pass some unfamiliar buildings, slowing down and repeating the Vietnamese phrase for "district headquarters" to peasants who keep pointing down the road.

Finally I stop at the building with the largest government flag in the area. The front office is filled with ancient wooden desks and young secretaries and clerks half asleep in the heat. I ask a girl near the counter for directions to the American district adviser's office.

She giggles, covering her mouth in embarrassment. Maybe she doesn't understand the question. I smile and wait a moment.

The rest of the people in the room avoid my eyes, looking out windows or down at paper on their desks.

I ask again, slowly. The girl giggles again. She motions toward a man. But he turns away and won't look at me. What is happening?

I walk to another counter. The clerk there is fixing the window shade, staring through the glass, fooling with the shutter. All around the room Vietnamese are looking the other way or busy with paper on their desks. I turn back to the girl.

"Could you please tell where the CORDS office is?" I say loudly to the group over her head. I can't believe that no one will answer.

No answer. Muted giggling and faces all around concentrating furiously on desk work. I am suddenly very aware of being an American, an outsider. This isn't a language problem. Someone is bound to know Bassford's name.

A minute passes in silence while I stand trying to find someone who'll look me in the eye. I get mad and walk into the middle of them, planting myself in front of one clerk in the center of the room, hands on my hips.

"Where is Mr. Bassford? Where is the American CORDS office?" I demand loudly.

The clerk looks up from his papers with a blank expression as if I'm not there. More silence. Then a voice behind me calls out in halting English.

"May I help you, sir?"

I repeat the question, and my rescuer, who has come out of a nearby office, points to a building outside the front door.

I thank him and walk out to find Bassford. Behind me, another wave of suppressed giggles passes across the room. I suddenly want to look in a mirror, or pinch myself, to make sure I really exist, and that I've spent nearly nine months in this part of the world.

Cu Chi

December 21

Cu Chi district is an hour's drive from Saigon. Until this month, an American base camp there, headquarters of the Twenty-fifth Division, housed nearly fourteen thousand GIs. Now the men have left and ARVN has both the base and full responsibility for the area's defense. The White House calls this process "Vietnamization," a clumsy word at best. One effect of Vietnamization is an economic depression wherever it happens. By leaving, the Americans deflate the job market: no more work in and around the base for local people. And GIs who patronize local businesses are gone, too.

I am driving to Cu Chi today to see what remains and to write about it. The land is flat and green and the sun is hot this time of year. Photographer Dick Swanson and his dark and beautiful Vietnamese wife, Germaine, are in the car and as we move along in the warm morning I am sleepily wishing the drive will continue . . . and continue, so I don't have to start work.

I did some research on the district yesterday. The people grow sweet potatoes, rice and bananas and raise livestock. Cu Chi district was named for a cu chi tree one hundred feet tall and seven feet wide, according to local records. It grew near a market and gathering spot in the capital. In 1946 after a fight with local resistance forces, the French army cut it down.

Some of Viet Nam's fiercest resistance fighters come from here. They joined the Cochin Chinese uprising in 1940 and have been fighting ever since. The area was solidly Viet Minh during the last war. In this one, the Vietcong controlled Cu Chi until 1965. Then the American camp was built, a flat, dusty fourteen-million-dollar complex of impressive machinery. In the years after that, the Americans fought all around the area. They called in air strikes, defoliated crops and cut up fields and jungles with combat-equipped bulldozers and heavy artillery.

Then last month they left.

Now we've passed district headquarters and we are looking for the town which usually grows up around American camps. Down the road we find a small shanty-town of laundries, brothels and deserted bars, hardly a community that could serve the base. It is small, we later find out, because its business is illicit. It has been off limits to GIs since 1968, so they must sneak off base to use the whorehouses or the one-day laundry service.

We stop at a farmhouse where a bony, bronzed old woman walks barefoot in some grain spread out on a mat. When you stop anywhere—you, the tall Westerner with Time-Life written on your jeep—it attracts attention. Half a dozen teen-agers pull up on Hondas. They wear sun-glasses, fatigue caps, and have tattoos and mottled teeth. Children gather. Old people stare out of doorways. Germaine talks to the lady and she is bitter. The Vietnamese government took half her farmland in 1965 for the American base. She blames the Americans for this. Now she has only two hectares (about five acres) left. She must share these with relatives. No one is making any money.

She worked at the base as a laundress and hooch (GI barracks) maid for a while, but the job ended a few months ago. She is forty, has seven children and works with her husband in the fields now. Her name is Tin Thi Ngan. Dick takes pictures, directing the children and neighbors to move this way or that. I watch this old woman, thinking how little I know of her life. She is proud and resents the American soldiers. But their money made a difference in her life. *What* difference?

"The Americans took away my land, then I had to work for them," she says in a low, unmoving peasant expression that masks everything to me. "Some of the work was hard, but the money was good and everybody had enough. Now it will be harder." Nothing more. Her life remains hidden from further prying.

We drive on. A roadside shed is empty: PAINTING, WASH CAR, MECHANICAL PUMP, PATCH TIRES. WE ARE SPECIALIST IN MILITARY—PERMANENT HOURS. A parking place for Hondas outside the base is now a muddy lot beside a rice paddy. We stop by the shed. Germaine notices people staring out of an old farmhouse.

The women and children in the doorway seem to me like figures in a picture of the 1930s Depression. Out of dust and passing days they watch the world push by them, powerless to shape or change it. We talk to a white-haired, wrinkled matriarch named Tran Thi Lieu. She never worked for the Americans, but their military operations have caused her trouble. Defoliation killed her mango and jackfruit trees. Her rice and bean harvest was bad because of American chemicals. American planes dropped flares at night, regularly setting her haystack on fire. Several neighbors' houses caught fire, too. Dick takes more pictures. We leave the house and walk toward the car. I am impressed by this tough, uncomplaining woman. She told us about her crop troubles only because we asked. Next year will be different, and the seasons will pass on.

Kids, again, are gathering around. They say they used to make money washing American trucks, so much that some quit school. Sometimes they were given enough military script to get a thousand piasters from the local money changer.

Most of the older boys, looking tough in sunglasses and fatigue caps, won't be going back to school. "Maybe later," says one kid named Cu, leaning against the car. "First I see if the Americans or other people coming back." I am thinking that soon Cu will be in Saigon hustling money.

Lunchtime. We drive into Cu Chi district town. Germaine picks a grimy little soup stall on the main road. The old woman cooking inside is friendly: a toothless broomstick behind a greasy stove with noodles and vegetables piled high. The stall is fitted with little stools and tables, and she stands in the middle of all this, up to her elbows in food and pots and pans, cooking and talking.

She and Germaine talk and she tells her she's cooked for Americans before. I ask to hear more about this. GI truck drivers came by in the morning for soup before going on the road, she says, smiling proudly, adding that they sometimes skipped lunch in Saigon in order to get back to her place to have a bowl in the afternoon.

Since the town was off limits, they usually ate in secret in a back room. A while ago, one group called her over after the meal.

"Mama," said one GI smiling and handing her two thousand piasters, "get some clothes."

Then they said goodbye and walked out.

"I haven't seen them for some weeks," she says, still up to her elbows in noodles and working steadily on our soup. "I think they have gone somewhere and will not be back." Germaine tells her they've gone back to America.

We drive toward the base again and stop at a laundry in the shanty town. Trach Tran Van, who is forty-eight and has thirteen kids, used to run a big business. The army provides GIs with free laundry service on base. But it takes three days, and Trach would clean and press uniforms in one day for any unit whose sergeant risked bringing them into town. Plenty did. The middleman's fee was worth it.

Trach is reading a novel in English by John O'Hara when we come in. He wears wire-rimmed glasses, and reminds me of Vietnamese reporters I see around the Saigon coffee shops. He has lost money because of the pullout. He holds unpaid bills totaling $270 from a departing aviation detachment. A particular sergeant who was the go-between—and is still in the area—won't pay the bills. And Trach has no way to collect. His business deals are against army regulations to begin with.

109

Trach's business brought in nine thousand piasters a month. Now he is raising pigs and chickens and shipping livestock feed in from Saigon for local farmers. He also has a generator and recharges batteries. So now he is making fifteen thousand piasters a month and everybody seems happy. Still, he wishes the American soldiers would pay their bills. So do I. I wish I could do something about this sergeant—how callously another American has slapped yet another Vietnamese in the face!

One last job. We have to interview some whores. There are still tin shacks with plastic flowers out front and girls hanging around. We pull into one house as some ARVN medics pull out. They've been giving penicillin shots. That answers one question about who'll pick up the slack in the vice trade.

The "house" is pathetic. A single room with a curtain hiding a bed in the corner. Several dumpy little girls are sitting inside. One has a pimple on her nose and bad teeth. She was a hooch maid and she lost her job when the Americans pulled out.

The prettiest girl has a thin face and stringy hair. A year ago, she met a GI in a camp near the coast, and she says she has a baby by him. She followed him up-country when he was transferred, then again to Cu Chi. Now he is gone. She has pictures of him and asks us to find him. She thinks he is at Long Binh post. In the picture he is beefy and looks as though he came from a farm. Clean cut and serious, not too bright. But he knew enough to ditch the girl, and she is getting red-faced and crying as she talks about him.

She gives me his address and I say I will write to tell him where to find her. (I do this a week later, and the letter is returned, saying no such person is at that address.)

We leave. The girl is smiling through tears at this thin bit of hope. There is nothing to do but get in the car and drive away. There are so *many* casualties in Viet Nam. This naïve girl's tears trickle down her face as if they were blood. And there is nothing I can do except drive away carrying a worthless address.

We stop at the American Pacification office on the way out. The army major in charge tells us that the district, about fifty thousand people, will probably go back to its subsistence farming way of life, the way it was before the Americans came.

Merry Christmas

December 25

A bad day so far. I left a somber party at 2:00 A.M., moody as hell. Then I sat cross-legged by my Christmas tree in the corner of the house, alone at 3:00 A.M., and opened a few presents from the folks, sent all the way from California. Some nice things; but when I turned around to thank them, no one was there.

Now I'm sitting on a folding chair in a sea of sun-burned GIs and Bob Hope is leaning on a golf club at Long Binh army post and telling a joke about a GI trying to convince a girl his two stripes mean he's a general. That way the girl will be impressed. Get it? Perhaps in Hope's time, GIs wanted to be generals. Now they want to go home.

He waves his golf club at us while Les Brown plays show tunes. And several times he lifts his fingers in the "V" sign, explaining it means "victory" to him, an "honorable" peace. I want to hoist my middle finger back.

He is a great showman, and I think it would be wrong to belittle the trouble he takes to entertain the troops each year: the chorus girls and snappy one-line jokes. But why doesn't he grow up? There is nothing honorable about this war, and most GIs aren't proud to fight in it. They are here because they didn't want to go to jail. It isn't a patriotic sacrifice to die here; it is a stupid mistake.

So Merry Christmas, Mr. Hope. We appreciate the women you've brought along to wiggle their fannies at us, and some of your jokes are funny, though some aren't. The band is rather old fashioned. And you act as if this is World War II, wearing that field jacket spotted with patches, stripes and stars. And that baseball cap, wow.

But if you look to the horizon, over the heads of an audience yet unborn when you first started touring, there are flocks of helicopters patrolling a wide defense corridor so you don't get a mortar in your lap. And most of the kids in the audience are stoned. You look like a Santa Claus of another age—toys and hollow laughter that won't do the job much longer.

For this show is yet another bit of shiny wrapping paper, like the cosmetic MACV briefings and ribbons they give away. It helps, again, to hide the awful package underneath so that Americans back home will continue to cheer their government's efforts overseas—despite protests from pacifists, disgruntled GIs and sometimes a moody reporter like me.

Chi Ba

Her name, which is a title and not really a name, means "third sister." She has six kids and her husband drives a taxi. He is short, smiles a lot and is losing his hair. She lives in a spare room off my kitchen filled with family pictures, joss sticks, a tiny shrine for her ancestors and a few personal things. She tiptoes around the house barefoot and is sometimes servile to a point that is embarrassing.

But it is an easy relationship. She does her job well—cooking, housekeeping, washing clothes—and I, in turn, treat her like the professional she is, bringing small gifts when I go to Hong Kong or other places, seeing she has the tools she needs and the time she wants to visit her family.

Sometimes she writes notes through a friend who speaks a little English. This one appeared at breakfast a few weeks ago:

> Dear My Boss:
> I inform you the food from Saigon market is very expensive. So if you awake very late in the morning, I cannot waiting you. If I come to the market late time, I cannot get fresh food. I am very pleasant if you will get all foods from American store. I will prepare your meal from the food from PX.
> Sincerely, Mrs. Cong.
> P.S. please get soap for laundry.

For several months after I arrived, I couldn't tell if Chi Ba was married or not, for she seemed to have few friends. But one morning at 4:00 A.M. after a late story, I found a taxi parked in the garage, and asked at the office about it.

"That is Chi Ba's husband," said Madame Nga, the accountant, brightly. "He comes at night to stay with her."

"Husband? Does she have kids?"

Madame Nga smiled and nodded.

I was stunned. "When does she see them? Who takes care of them?"

"She visits them on Sundays, and sometimes they come to the house when you are not there."

I told Madame Nga to have Chi Ba invite her kids and husband over any time she wanted, that I would enjoy having them visit. Result: a much cheerier household. I also got presents at Christmas and Tet—a porcelain ashtray shaped like a lobster and four brass faces mounted on a black wooden base. Rather unusual. And finally, I'm getting a paunch from Chi Ba's cooking, so I guess everyone is happy.

7

News comes and goes, water rushing against rocks then pulling back. The periods between can be unsettling. You play some tennis, chase a girl or two, see friends. But the weight of time moving slowly is crushing. You start looking over your shoulder worrying, wondering what you are missing. . . .

We work seven days a week in Saigon. My week lurches toward collapse between midnight Saturday and dawn Sunday as the editors, twelve hours behind on the other side of the world, close the magazine. "Checking" queries keep us in, or near, the office much of the night. Then to bed about sunrise, rolling out in the afternoon for a swim, supper and maybe a Sunday night movie at the MACV compound. That was the weekend. The long weeks have been slow lately, but that is about to change.

Laos Coming

For a week, Jon has sensed something about Laos. He talks of going there in a hot, urgent way. Soon everyone in the bureau feels it. Then tonight MACV's information people call us three times trying to reach someone else. We tell them it's a wrong number and go back to work.

They've accidentally called every news bureau in town except us to announce a major briefing. Jon is furious. We've lost twenty-four hours. However, the briefing is embargoed, which means we can't report what they tell us. And then adding to the surrealism, there's an embargo on the embargo.

That means we can't communicate anything at all to our editors. It is late in the week, and Saigon is wild with speculation. Ever since the Cambodian invasion, we've talked about the other shoe dropping. Nothing to do but wait.

Show Business

January 30

The briefing is at 6:00 P.M. It is limited to one correspondent from each bureau. Jon goes, and he is treated to a classic military show—incomplete information, double entendres, outright lies, hostile briefers.

The first briefer says that American troops started moving yesterday across South Viet Nam's northern frontier toward Laos. Fine, but are they *going* to Laos?

No comment.

Another military officer steps forward and talks about the Ho Chi Minh trail, which is mostly in Laos. He explains trail routes, talks about troops and supplies coming down them, briefs reporters on U.S. "interdiction" (bombing) missions designed to stop that flow. He says that unusually large quantities of troops and supplies have come down the trail lately and have moved into South Viet Nam's upper military regions.

Fine. Does that mean the Vietnamese army, covered by American planes and helicopters, is going into Laos to cut the trail? No, says the briefer. The "allied" forces will stop short of the border, turn left, and head south for the Ashau Valley, which is controlled in part by North Vietnamese troops.

But why is a huge military force, perhaps as many as twenty thousand men, bothering to march across the northern provinces and make an inefficient detour?

Diversionary tactics, says the briefer, straight-faced.

Then he says MACV will have a press center at Quang Tri. That is hundreds of miles from the Ashau Valley, convenient for covering an invasion of Laos but hardly a place to watch the Ashau.

What about Vietnamese operations?

We can't speak for the Vietnamese, says the "allied" briefer. That policy will plague us throughout the operation—which, of course, is indeed going into Laos. And it will cost the life of at least one dear friend.

Quang Tri

January 31

I have to go north. Regular hitches are off. The shuttle planes flying in that direction are on emergency status. But during yesterday's briefing MACV offered us a bone ("We are taking you into our confidence," a MACV colonel said, "because this is what you people have been asking for."), and arranged rides on planes heading directly for Quang Tri.

I am suited up in field gear. Backpack, camera, raincoat, typewriter, chocolate bars in one pocket, notebook— and the usual fear of flying those wobbly C-130s. The trip starts with a leg south to Cantho to get cargo. A lone GI gets on with the machinery and several of us ask him what his orders say. He's got temporary duty in Quang Tri for ninety days. That's all he knows. I read a book, try to sleep, worry a little.

It gets colder as we fly north. Quang Tri's runway is loose steel planking and it sounds like chains rattling as we land and roll over it. Outside the plane, it is like winter in Iowa. I can see my steamy breath. The airstrip is almost shaking with noise and activity, mostly the loud grinding of airplane engines, the planes landing and taking off five minutes apart with wispy strips of exhaust hanging behind them.

The countryside is gray, wet and cold, and wintry, as if we left the tropics years ago. Combat-equipped GIs in parkas move through the air terminal looking like actors from an Arctic war movie. A truck arrives from the information office and takes us through a series of muddy roads to some barracks which will become the press center.

Reporters are still embargoed. We can take notes but can not file stories. So we set up bunks, find the mess hall, get some coffee, check the telephones, pull gear together for the morning when helicopters will be heading west. Quang Tri is a jumping-off point. The story this week is on the road between here and Laos—a cold, misty wilderness stretching west along Route Nine toward mountains and jungles in Laos.

The chopper pad, extending the length of several football fields, is already alive with machinery: Slick, Cobra and Loch birds pumping their propeller blades in the snappy air, sounding like thousands of cupped hands clapping. The sounds are forbidding and dramatic in the cold sunset, talking of death and unhappiness to come.

The Last Invasion

February 3

Laos may be a finale: the last big push by American troops in Indochina before they go home. The operation is called Dewey Canyon II, and for public relations reasons it will later be given a Vietnamese title, Lam Son 719. But it is an American effort, planned by Americans and sponsored by American money. And it is a stormy controversy—the biggest since the invasion of Cambodia. As it begins, troops move in huge columns along a highway stretching across the northern tip of South Viet Nam. It is rainy and cold as I catch a chopper out of Quang Tri, and the skies have been gray for days.

"That's Route Nine," says the chopper pilot named Forbes, banking the bird sideways so I can look down at the concrete road stretching toward Laos. Forbes says he likes his work. I am sitting behind him, looking at "I am the God of Hellfire" painted on the back of his helmet. The morning fog is heavy, so we are flying about fifty feet above the road, taking the curves like a racing car as the flat, misty countryside rises westward toward tall mountains.

Forbes is showing off a bit.

We fly over long columns of trucks moving toward Firebase Vandergrift about twenty miles away. The helicopter dips down to the road, then bounces up again like a rubber ball, jerking and quivering in the air. I'm crowded into the back seat with a machine gun and a box of ammunition looking out the window. At Vandergrift, the highway becomes a dirt road and the country changes to jagged rock formations—hills, forests, canyons and white rivers.

"That's real Indian country," says Forbes enthusiastically, motioning north. "We had a couple of kills up there just two days ago." All I can see is the back of his helmet—but I am convinced this rather pedestrian "god" and I would not get along.

We pass over Vandergrift, a muddy plain filled with trucks, tanks and GIs. Big Chinooks hover overhead like pterodactyls, carrying equipment which hangs by long cables swaying in the wind.

Route Nine has moved into mountains now. Two convoy trucks are overturned on a hairpin curve. A GI sits in a third, still upright, surveying the damage and waiting, arms folded dejectedly, to be rescued. He glances up noncommittally as we circle, and I look down at him and his trucks. He is a picture in a book on existentialism: trapped en route to the invasion, late again; meanwhile metal men pass by preparing for an insane ritual that will decide who owns the southeastern corner of Laos this year, which is assumed to be highly valuable property.

We climb toward Khe Sanh plateau. A slender waterfall shoots off one mountain, and the fog on the plateau looks like gray factory smoke.

Forbes drops us on the steel-planking airstrip, built by marines in 1968. It is punctured by jagged mortar holes from former battles. I wave good-bye without saying anything about his helmet, and he lifts off. The plateau is dusty. Road graders roll back and forth across the clay where two more airstrips will be built to suport the Laos invasion. GIs working around me mark holes in the old planking with white strips of cloth. These show where shells are buried from the marines' stand in 1968. Welders work on the old planks that are damaged. Jackhammers rattle, and the droning of field generators mixes with the clatter of Chinooks raising hundred-foot clouds of red dust as they hover.

I talk to a Major supervising the construction work. He slept here last night. "The fog rolls in and goes right through you," he says, hugging a cup of coffee. All around the windy plateau GIs are digging deep holes to sleep in.

I walk over to one platoon and a fat sergeant with curly hair and a West Virginia twang sees my camera and notebook. "You should have been here yesterday," he says enthusiastically. "My truck hit a mine. It blew a man's leg off."

I am standing by the hole wondering what he expects me to do. Write a story? The sergeant motions to an embarrassed kid digging another hole nearby.

"That's the driver, there."

Okay, sarge. A voice inside me is bouncing between walls and getting louder, trying to get out. We'll do a story titled "that-was-the-kid-who-drove-the-truck . . . etc." And we'll send it to his hometown paper.

Lunchtime. I see a couple of GIs near the soup kitchen. Something about them. They are loose, maybe stoned. We talk—they are from Spanish Harlem—and they invite me to eat at their campfire. C rations and chocolate bars, some gleeful talk about their stash, and questions about The World (the United States—home). One guy named Baez—tough, humorous, big hands—was on Firebase Ripcord last summer when the North Vietnamese overran it.

"You could see them coming over the hill," he says, telling how he was on the last chopper out. "And then this guy"—Baez makes a big motion with his hands—"put that NVA flag right in the ground . . . wow!"

Baez says the younger men were the last ones out. "It's the draftees who get it," he concludes bitterly, "not the lifers."

At the plateau's west end, an armored column moves out for Lang Vei, the forward headquarters three miles from Laos. I stand by the road, thumb out, and a GI leans out of a five-ton wrecker and motions me in. This is Butch. His name is painted on the side of the truck. The driver's name is Frenchy—his name is on the other side. Both are draftees, one from California, the other from Kentucky.

They are dusty, lean teen-agers with moustaches and they like having a guest. Butch climbs in the back and brings me a bottle of sherry, then rum. He brings out Cokes, cigars, chocolate and then produces his stash, Cambodian red. We wind around muddy curves, past huge bomb craters, and splash through stream beds, and I am caught up in the masculine music of it, the sounds of heavy machinery, helicopters overhead, drinking rum, smoking cigars and watching Butch roll a joint.

Elephant grass forms a green wall on each side of the road, and the column goes slowly. Butch holds out the joint. "Try this," he grins, and dips it into a tiny bottle of mint flavoring stolen from the mess hall. Frenchy keeps on driving. At one point the road drops dizzily into a deep stream bed. The stream plunges off a cliff inches from our wheels. We are drinking and talking—and stoned—and enjoying the ride.

"Just think," grins Frenchy as he shifts gears. "If it's sunny tomorrow, we might get to see the Laotian border." It seems very funny at the time.

Lang Vei is freshly cut-up forest. Bulldozers pull trees out of the ground. GIs are digging holes in case the North Vietnamese in the hills send rockets during the night. I am introduced to a colonel who worked in the area ten years ago. He looks like an old boxer weathered and pummeled by life, and he blinks as he talks.

"We drove up here regularly," he says, smiling at the memory. "There were elephants and cobras then, and the Montagnard women were bare breasted." What about the war? "A few Pathet Lao were in the area. We'd meet with the Royal Laotian forces, feed them, and tell them to get their asses back and fight."

I am thinking about old soldiers as he talks, and how they never die.

About sundown, a kid stumbles on the sunken opening to a tunnel complex. Everybody gathers around while a

GI with a gun and flashlight, roped like a mountain climber, is lowered into the entrance. He has a dog, and it goes in first. Another guy backs him up. "Tunnel rats" they are called: a minute of tension, then they find the passage is empty.

Darkness. Butch cooks a can of spaghetti and meatballs on a gasoline stove "borrowed" from the Quang Tri mess hall. We add coffee, chicken soup, crackers and chocolate bars from the C-rations kits. As the food simmers, the night is lit by napalm fires in the hills above us where American planes are trying to hit the Communist positions. The talk, as usual, centers around The World. We roll out sleeping bags under Butch and Frenchy's truck and doze off, hoping the rockets won't come.

The morning's first noise is General Hill, the field commander, yelling at a GI to put on his helmet. I am sleepily wishing someone would throw a rock at the general's head. I say good-bye to Butch and Frenchy, and, after breakfast, start out for the last stop, the old Lang Vei special forces camp near the border. From there you can see the Pong River, which separates Viet Nam from Laos.

North Vietnamese in Russian-built tanks overran the camp in 1968, catching the Green Berets asleep one night and driving their big guns right on top of the camp. Pieces of the battle still litter the hillside—old armored carriers, burned out Russian tanks, half-buried bunkers. I ride up with a small engineering convoy. Just before the camp, we detour to avoid a live five-hundred-pound-bomb in the road. Then we climb a steep hill.

The camp is on a high bluff overlooking the river. American soldiers are burning the tall grass, which fuels my sense of drama as the smoke drifts across the old tanks and bunkers. An armored cavalry unit has made camp and one kid's helmet says, "Laos?" Spotter planes and Cobra gunships fly overhead. The sky is filled with ominous clatter.

A road cut through the brush leads downhill from the camp to a river tributary. A GI named Bob Phillips offers to walk down with me. He doesn't carry weapons and neither do I. "Hey, man, take *something*," says one GI, holding out an M-16. But we smile and say no, and they make signs like we are crazy.

They know Bob won't. He has refused to carry a gun for six months. He avoids court-martial by doing his assigned jobs well—operating equipment, running errands. And me? I vowed long ago that I wouldn't carry a gun *and* a notebook in this war. They don't mix and I prefer the notebook. I would rather run than shoot back. I admit it. And I think that men who go to jail to avoid killing people in war are brave, not cowardly.

Bob is a loner. He keeps to himself and smiles strangely when he talks as though he knows something I don't. He probably smokes grass, but he was a cop in civilian life and seems an odd mixture of rebellion and conventional attitudes. And he is lonely. He tells stories one after another as we walk to the river, as though no one has listened for a long time.

At the river a crew of GIs in an armored carrier is stuck in the mud, cursing and waiting for another carrier to pull them out. Others are bathing and splashing water around. I ask one GI about Nixon's pledge that Americans will stay out of Laos. "Don't worry," he jokes, "this is Vietnamese water."

For now, this is the closest I can get to the border. Bob and I walk up the hill to Lang Vei again and I arrange to ride with another convoy back to the main camp. Bob sits on a tree stump playing an old guitar as we pull out. He holds up the "V" sign.

Invasion Day

I get up early. The chopper pad is windy and confused. Every bird is moving and going to Khe Sanh or nearby. I wave thumbs up and catch a Slick assigned to a combat assault team. The bird will be picking up ARVN troops from fire bases near the border and carrying them into Laos.

It is windy and the team flies in tight formation. I sit cross-legged on the floor of my chopper, looking down, trying to appear unmoved as we seem to be tossed about in the wind like a Ping-Pong ball. Up . . . down . . . choppers gyrating wildly in relation to one another. The mountains ahead are huge waves we are being washed into. The other helicopters press in, rocking, drifting too close. Each time, this startles me. I keep trying to slam my foot on an imaginary brake and veer away. Finally Khe Sanh appears. Its flatness is comforting.

The landing is not. Hundreds of helicopters are in motion here, roaring and raising dust. The plateau is covered with flying machines in long rows, blades drawing hundreds of circles in the snappy morning air. I feel like I am being dropped into a hurricane. The wind whips off my sunglasses. I stumble to my knees, pushed sideways then forward by rotor wash, backpack and camera flopping about. I can't see and my boots slip on the sand. I trip on little hills and fall into ditches as our ragged group, heads in our hands, stumbles from chopper to chopper asking for rides to the border.

Nothing. The pilots on combat assaults are forbidden to take journalists along. And if they aren't flying combat missions, they have orders not to take us anywhere at all. I give up in disgust and walk down the road toward the base camps at Ham Nghi and Lang Vei. The sky is filled with gunships: dark, hawk-nosed machines with big rocket pods.

I catch a truck going to the border. We pass ARVN headquarters at Ham Nghi. Long lines of little men in jungle suits cradling big American M-16s wait for choppers at the landing zones. From a distance they resemble mechanical men—then suddenly I see tiny robots walking stiffly like toy soldiers into a wall of flame, screaming in human voices as they are consumed. The truck stalls in a traffic jam and I jump out impatiently and walk several hundred yards down the road.

Suddenly I am very alone. Two Vietnamese soldiers walk by, looking strangely at me. I sit down and wait nervously for a truck—anything! Nothing comes for half an hour.

Finally, a pickup filled with Vietnamese drives up. I wave anxiously and it stops. A Vietnamese reporter for *The New York Times* is in the back, and he asks the driver to give me a lift. He smiles. I smile back. He nods. Relieved, I climb in and the truck churns around curves and through heavy dust to the border.

The invasion began at 7:42 A.M. There was little to see at the time. Tanks with Vietnamese soldiers sitting on top, tree branches attached for camouflage, crossed the border with no resistance. They are still doing this when I arrive, engines growling and treads clanking. The border is lined with encamped American and Vietnamese artillery units, surrounded by war's sickening ecological side effects—paper and metal garbage, smoky cooking fires, cardboard and candy wrappers strewn about, cracker-box outdoor toilets, rusty shell casings piled up, the funky smell of C rations and rice cooking over the fires. All around here are bones of bushes and trees burned away to discourage snipers.

The *Times* man and I walk to the border. Two ARVN MPs in a jeep call out when we reach the signpost marker (WARNING: NO U.S. PERSONNEL BEYOND THIS POINT). My friend turns and smiles, shows his press card. With a little arm waving and some tricky multitonal Vietnamese linguistics, he convinces them we are authorized to cross.

Then we look at each other. Do we *really* want to do this? What the hell, I am thinking. I have to see Laos, don't I?

We walk into Laos, unarmed, alone, watching ahead and saying nothing for about fifteen minutes. It is a risky thing to do. But I can't resist doing it. It is very quiet. The road is rimmed now by high walls of grass and thicket. We see nothing—no one anywhere. A few helicopters fly overhead, but there is no way of telling what is off the road. An easy place to get hurt. We round one corner, then another. I am getting nervous. I look for high ground, hoping to see the column of tanks ahead to get a sense of the invasion's physical shape. Another helicopter flies by. We suddenly face each other, frightened. We turn around.

Ironically, a tank column rumbles by a few minutes later, clanking on to some inferno I can't envision. The men, twigs tied to their helmets, crowd together on top of the tanks. They are hidden behind larger branches, like children on a small wooded hill gathered for a picnic. Lemonade and chicken salad? I tell the voice inside me to shut up.

I snap pictures, and a few men wave. According to the briefing we've gotten, they will move down Route Nine in a flying wedge. Ranger units ahead, followed and flanked by armor. Vietnamese marines tailgate, and airborne units are nine kilometers north. The ARVN Ninth Division is five kilometers south of the column.

The North Vietnamese aren't likely to fight now. They'll attack when the Southerners are settled in static positions with extended supply lines. Each ARVN base will be softened by mortars, then harassed by sappers. Ground attacks will follow. Other North Vietnamese will harass the tank column on Route Nine with land mines and shoot down American helicopters flying in to resupply the bases.

And back in Saigon the official briefers will turn ARVN's defeats into victories with half truths and inflated statistics. For now, my friend and I walk again to the border, past the American sign and the Vietnamese MPs, and catch a ride to Khe Sanh. I am thinking of chicken salad and hurricanes and dust and how glad I am not to be a Vietnamese soldier.

All the News

Sunday morning and the magazine is closing in New York with this week's version of the Laos invasion. We've been up all night checking copy, and An is here to help with last-minute problems.

He casually mentions that ARVN's Third Airborne Brigade commander, a full colonel, was captured when the North Vietnamese overran a firebase in Laos the other day. It's an important item.

An knew about it yesterday. But he didn't say anything, because his horoscope advised him to remain silent on matters of importance. Fortunately the stars said to give advice and reveal important information to friends and colleagues today, so we got the news.

My Friend, The Hired Killer

The war across the border goes badly. That word comes from the helicopter pilots who are my best sources at Khe Sanh. They know ARVN is in trouble, for many of the firebases they fly into are surrounded and taking heavy fire. Some bases are being overrun.

Trouble is easy to spot: heavy medivac traffic and anti-aircraft fire so fierce that supply ships can't get in. And it means helicopters going down.

There is a pool, five dollars from each crew to the ship returning from Laos with the most bullet holes. If it crashes coming home, no prize.

I hear stories. A Loch pilot, a first lieutenant, was circling low the other day on a scouting mission when he flew over a company of North Vietnamese. They opened fire, and a bullet burst through the cabin floor hitting the pilot in the face. It blew his brains out. Blood and skull tissue splattered over the cabin, and the crew chief, who isn't trained to fly, grabbed the controls. He was nearly blinded by the blood, but kept aloft, leaning out the window to steer. He flew shakily back to ARVN Firebase Aloui and crash landed, surviving.

I've been visiting Alpha battery of the Seventy-seventh Aerial Rocket Artillery Battalion. The pilots fly Cobras—shark-nosed birds with pods that shoot large rockets or showers of darts. The Cobra attacks like a fighter plane, circling a target until called down by a ground controller. Then it dives in a terrifying rush, spewing rocket fire at its victims.

The Seventy-seventh men are friendly, and they talk openly. I spend the most time with a fellow from New Orleans named Fred. He is tough, salty, solidly built—archetypal American mythology. He dropped out of college during the sixties to join the Green Berets. In that capacity he's been, among other things, a deep-sea diver, mountain climber, combat-trained skier. During an earlier tour of Viet Nam he "advised" a Vietnamese reconnaissance team which ran missions he still won't talk about. On the side, he ran a sixty-bed hospital. He is a trained medic.

To me, Fred personifies much of what is good and evil in America. Put him in a hospital and he saves lives. As a helicopter pilot he takes them. He is sentimental (he's reading *Love Story* this week) and he even likes to cook for friends occasionally. He also plays cards, drinks beer and curses heavily. There is implicit violence in his eyes as he talks. The eyes are blue, and he has a thin uneven moustache.

I ask him one morning why he flies Cobras. He is sitting on his bunk and laughs, squeezing a beer can between calloused hands. "Lack of better things to do," he starts. Then he looks at the ground, unused to examining himself. "More money, I guess. I tried damn near everything else the army had." He has seen a lot of war and sees it mostly in nationalistic terms. "If there weren't any American pilots involved in this operation," he snorts, looking around as he talks, "I'd just as soon go home."

He once wanted to go all the way, invade and bomb Hanoi, for a World War II–style victory. Now he thinks the war is a "big waste."

I spend several days with him, fascinated but knowing we can never be friends. I like him. There is a raucous, thoroughly alive human being peering through his hard soldier-of-fortune exterior. Yet this spirit is completely linked with a technology that is antilife. We talk, and we talk honestly. But it is another of the half relationships which journalism rides piggyback on. I have to get close to Fred for a moment in time to write about him. That's all.

Still, there is much in him, his need for adventure, his sense of manhood, that I relate to. But again: we get close only because I have an article to write. A working connection. He gets to parade before twenty million readers; I get a job done.

I ask him one day on the chopper pad—trying not to be ridiculous or trite about it—how he feels about killing.

"Normally, you don't see who you are shooting at," he says with a shrug, leaning against his helicopter on the oily pad a hundred yards from his tent. "You're given a direction and you deliver fire."

I ask if he thinks about the people on the ground. He looks at me. Then he looks away, groping for something he prefers not to think about.

"Not really. When the paperwork comes down and you get accredited with kills, you feel good. You did your job well. This is what you are trained for, what you plan for."

He stops again, shrugs, and turns his eyes to meet mine. "You just get in and do it." He takes his helmet and climbs into the Cobra cockpit, ready for another run, and I wave as he closes the canopy. I am thinking, yes, the answer to war and other troubling questions for most of us is, indeed, that you don't think about it. You just do it. Morality means *nothing* more than that.

Dear Somebody

It is 8:30 P.M. in Khe Sanh and I'm sitting in the press tent trying to write you a letter in the semidarkness, having nothing else to do in this vacuum.

There isn't enough light to read by. And there is nowhere to go. The night air is a noisy mix of generators whining, occasional sputtering late helicopters and perimeter flares popping. The flares whizz up into the darkness, pop bright orange and float to the ground by parachute every few minutes.

Last night the other side laid some rockets and mortars on us, which added to the sounds. A convoy near one of the outer camps was ambushed first, and a lot of big guns opened up while we all scurried to bunkers. It lasted about half an hour. There were no more attacks in the night.

Khe Sanh is a noisy, dusty, melodramatic place. Heavy machinery and somber GIs, planes landing all the time, mountains all around. The choppers fill the air like a shifting cloud of insects, and there is dust, dust, and more dust. You are caked in it; it makes your hair impossible to comb, your clothes and boots filthy. It lends a sense of dime-novel staging to the whole thing: death, sweat and tough language, drama, combat, weapons and finally unending dust to cover all that is and will be done here.

I'm writing a story on chopper pilots. I've spent two days so far with the men I'm profiling. One is a Cobra gunship pilot—a tough, unblinking killer honest enough to admit he likes his work. The other is a blond GI from Missouri. He wears glasses and is quiet and unassuming, very middle class. He flies a convoy lift-ship. He gets shot at occasionally, and during our talks seemed to

137

take it all in stride, as if he were driving a truck through heavy traffic. War is truely insane—imagine saying in New York that you enjoy the company of a gunship pilot who likes to shoot rockets at people.

Yesterday I looked inside a chopper just back from Laos. It was filled with blood, and as I walked away from it up the road to the press camp, which overlooks the plateau, I impulsively turned and said to the vista below: "War is *shit*, people. Do you hear me?"

I stopped and looked out at the camp. And then I yelled it.

"DO YOU HEAR ME? I SAID WAR IS SHIT! IT'S ALL BULLSHIT!"

I yelled this a few more times until my throat was sore. Then I went to the field mess for dinner.

In three weeks I'll have been in Viet Nam for one year. I hear I'm being sent next to New York, and I admit I'll be damn glad to leave this place. It's been the best and worst year of a lifetime—an experience of bewildering parts, some cutting, others smooth like polished stones. I've written some important stories, I hope. The women, slight or serious, were unforgettable and the people of Asia have shown me so much about living. But there has been pain and waste and tragedy this year, and I can only guess how deeply the war has pressed into me. A year was enough. Let me at the States, American women, hamburger stands and hot rods. All that matters now is change.

Larry Burrows

Larry had waited three days for the ride. Then, unshaven with bloodshot eyes from lack of sleep, he climbed into the Vietnamese helicopter with three other photographers to shoot airborne pictures of the Laotian campaign. The choppers wound up and sputtered and kicked up dust and lifted off.

And now he is gone. The helicopter—and another carrying four Vietnamese army officers—flew over a mountaintop antiaircraft concentration by mistake. They drew fire and one helicopter exploded in midair, plunging in smoke and fire to the earth. The other, ahead, somehow turned and came back into the flack. A direct hit sliced off its tail boom and main rotor shaft, and it crashed and burned.

Our bitterness is unbounded. The American command for weeks has refused to let reporters hitch rides with the hundreds of American helicopters coming and going across the border. The usual unspoken reason: if reporters and cameramen can't see the action, the public might accept the lies told at official briefings. For the South Vietnamese are losing, and the Pentagon wants to hide this.

So we turned to Vietnamese helicopters. It was risky, for Vietnamese air force pilots are new to chopper technology. They get lost easily. And they don't know where the antiaircraft guns are located across the border. They have about a dozen choppers up here, mostly for transporting generals.

Larry Burrows was easily one of the best and bravest men to take pictures in Viet Nam, and he was among the first to get permission to ride with them. He and Kent Potter of UPI, a bold and tough photographer I knew briefly in Cambodia, Henri Huet of AP and a Japanese free-lancer named Keisaburo Shimamoto left Ham Nghi with three other helicopters, one in the lead carrying an ARVN general. Jon Larsen and Ron Ridenhour, a freelance reporter and friend, were in the one that returned. But the others fell behind and strayed off course.

An American spotter plane flying near the mountains tried to warn the choppers away at the last moment. But it was too late. He could only radio Khe Sanh and tell of the death scene.

In my memory, Larry is a tall, angular Englishman, craggy-faced with thick glasses and a pleasant clip to his words. He is justly famous. There are more stories of him rushing toward bullets or standing up under fire to get a better camera angle than I can count. He could do anything well, and had taken pictures of Hemingway and Angkor Wat and countless other subjects for *Life* magazine in his career. But he was most famous—and respected—for his combat photography.

And he was a friend. In Cambodia, he could see I was new and frightened, and though I never asked, he would talk of what he'd seen in the field, offer advice and thoughts about the war. It was a courtesy, very British and very human. He was thoroughly professional but he didn't mind telling me what he knew, and I needed his help and was deeply grateful for it.

He was often in Saigon, always friendly, always steeped in his work. Before that helicopter ride, he'd camped on the border for several days to photograph the first tanks going across on invasion day. Friends said he'd looked worn and tired at Ham Nghi, bloodshot eyes over a three-day beard, a dirty towel around his neck, cameras dangling heavier than usual.

And now he is gone—in part, fate. But also because the Pentagon kept us from the American pilots, who might have avoided the antiaircraft guns. I am bitter, and I am wishing the men responsible for that policy could have taken the ride with him.

Press Problems

Dealing with the American military has never been easy. The generals and their underlings often regard journalists as leftists, hippies, antiwar spies—or at least upstarts who lack the proper respect for the military's role as defenders of America.

More important, the military has long been convinced that uncensored press coverage hurts the American position here. "There is within the military a very real conviction that the war effort has been hampered and, indeed, hurt by the press," Marsh Clark observed in a 1969 story written from Saigon. ". . . Newsmen are considered to be pacifists, sensationalists, peaceniks and, even worse, civilians who know nothing about military affairs."

Another friend, a former *Time* correspondent named John Mecklin, who served several years in America's Saigon embassy during the Diem era, made a similar point in his book *Mission in Torment,* which both criticized and defended the Saigon press corps. "A major foreign policy was wrecked, in part," he wrote, "by unadorned reporting of what was going on."

The military, of course, can hit back by giving out selective information which supports its position—or by giving out none at all. During this year I've been lied to so often that half truths have become an accepted fact of life. Just do the stories; let the lies roll off your back like the daily monsoon rains. Save your anger for a corner table at the bar or a dinner party among friends.

But Laos is different. The Pentagon's information policies helped kill a friend of mine. All along, we knew the invasion was largely planned and paid for by MACV. It was monitored by American "advisers" who moved back and forth between command posts; it was supported by American helicopters and artillery. And it cost American lives. Infantrymen died during its early stages; American helicopter pilots were killed during the invasion itself.

Yet the American command consistently gave us only limited information about its role in Laos. When a helicopter went down, for example, nothing was reported unless it was lost. Those rescued or salvaged were not counted in official statistics. So if MACV announced in a week that fifty helicopters were shot down, it meant that at least a hundred had crashed.

Worst of all, the American command refused to brief us on "allied" activity, claiming that Laos was an ARVN operation. And that was that. Until Larry Burrows' death, we accepted this angrily, but short of rage. But now our frustration is personal. I'd been to more worthless press briefings in Quang Tri than I care to remember and had returned to Saigon to write another story. One that I missed the day after Larry died sums up much of our unhappiness with the American military. Here are some notes from Ron Ridenhour:

> The briefing was tense and quiet. The American briefer gave a terse rundown of the day's activities, and when the questions started they were biting and direct. Every night he had promised that tomorrow an ARVN briefer would be provided. But now it was twelve days after the operation had begun. The command still refused to comment on ARVN operations in Laos, and journalists were very effectively being barred from entering the battle zone.
>
> "Colonel," said one newsman angrily. "This situation is absolutely intolerable. The ARVN command posts are filled with U.S. advisers. They are manning radios, and dashing about delivering messages and getting their heads together. The operation couldn't have been undertaken without massive U.S. support and backing.
>
> "The American people are clearly paying for this venture and the American command is clearly running the whole show. You are deliberately not providing us with any relevant information about what is happening in

Laos, choosing instead to hide behind this very transparent façade of diplomatic and military protocol. Why, Colonel?"

The colonel repeated that the operation was an ARVN show and the United States could not comment on it.

The next day, everybody trudged out to the chopper pads to catch rides to Khe Sanh. If you couldn't get into Laos, you at least got as close as you could. Maybe you might stumble across something. Then around 3:00 that afternoon, word started filtering through press corps ranks that the long awaited ARVN briefing had finally materialized.

It was to be given at 4:30 P.M. in Quang Tri by none other than General Lam, Vietnamese I Corps commander, the man in charge of the operation. Newsmen scrambled aboard Quang Tri–bound choppers, eager to get something they could sink their teeth into.

"Even if he tells us nothing but bald-faced lies," said one, "it's gotta be more than we're getting now."

"Sure," another quipped. "But when we get there Lam won't be around. We'll get an ARVN briefer who'll have nothing to say."

He was right. An ARVN major marched in to address the gathered press corps smiling broadly. One would guess he was happy to be there.

"Lady and gentlemen," he began. "I, Major Hoi. I used to be from ARVN psy-war block. I here to help every people. I very glad to be here."

Then, grinning like a kid in a candy shop, Major Hoi delivered his prophesized bomb.

"I have order from General Lam to tell you this meeting canceled."

"Why was this meeting called?" exploded one network correspondent.

"I, Major Hoi. I used to be information officer, I Corps. I here to tell you meeting canceled."

Some laughed, some fought, but everyone threw in the towel after about ten minutes of listening to Major Hoi repeat who he was and how glad he was to be here.

The regular MACV briefing two hours later was about the same.

"Not much today," said the colonel. "Let me put it this way—no casualties, no damage."

143

Someone asked if Firebase Vandergrift had been mortared the night before. Yes, it had. Shouldn't that have been in the briefing? Yes, it should have been.

What about the F-4 Phantom jet shot down this morning? MACV didn't have an official report yet. What about the two choppers knocked down in the same place today?

"Gee, I don't know if we've got a report on that yet."

And at this point, Ron notes, the press briefing ended, give or take a few denials, evasions and outright lies. Journalism, indeed, is an adversary process. Soldiers and diplomats, who live off public money, somehow assume the public should be kept ignorant of what they do with it. Reporters generally have an opposing point of view, and the longer I stay in Viet Nam the more I am absolutely sure we are right.

Winning the War

We are banned again. The Vietnamese government, that cradle of developing democracy, has stopped three shipments of *Time* magazine at customs in recent weeks. For the magazine is reporting that the Laos campaign is going badly—horribly, in fact—and they don't want it to get around.

I admit it—I'm delighted. Our stories are solid, and they were difficult to get. We've had trouble finding reliable information. Then trouble with sources, the Vietnamese government, MACV. Then even with our editors, who were influenced at first by optimistic Pentagon assessments. And finally trouble with our office staff, whose faces fell steadily as the bad news came in. Our best information came from An's Vietnamese intelligence sources. Now he is taking abuse from other Vietnamese in the office for passing it on. The office is tense.

And now the presidential palace is upset with us. "*Time* magazine has always been high with the government," says a worried Vietnamese friend. "But the magazine is regarded as antigovernment now. President Thieu is very displeased."

Somehow, I can't stop smiling. We did a good job. To hell with Thieu.

8

Seen from space, the earth is serene: calm and blue and set clearly against the darkness of infinity. Tension is evident only in storm clouds, volatile masses of gray racing above the continents and oceans. If measured against the galaxy, they are minor spasms. Yet on the ground, viewed through a man's eyes, each storm threatens holocaust. A final explosion, and the earth is gone.

I tell myself, writing this, that Laos was a benign storm. That my country's men and machines will leave Asia now, taking with them the maverick energy disturbing this part of the earth. That the Asians will then settle this conflict untroubled by Western armies and foreign policy designs.

But this is illusory. For our bloated planes rise with bombs to seed further storms. And we have created and left behind new armies of ambitious men, "Vietnamized" Vietnamese; and the North, pledged in blood and ideology to fight on, will not rest until Viet Nam is reunited. So the storms will continue, threatening always to unleash one last explosion.

If this happens, we shall not escape. For our life-force is intermingled with this country now as if Southeast Asia were a living appendage. The small body is linked to the larger by catheters—transfusions of young men sent, then recycled, leaving blood, weaponry and bastard children behind. The men return to America each year in increasing confusion and discontent: drug use rises among them, discipline is down. Some go to graves, forgotten by an electorate once eager for war. And those alive, coming *home, find an unsympathetic society with few jobs and little glory. As the years pass this cycle of despair and wasted resources seems to grow as each man crosses the ocean, rising inside each of us until sometime, soon perhaps, the price will be exacted for what we have done.*

Coming Down

March 23

Journalism is often ugly, for the best stories are about disaster: war, poverty, back-room politics, plague. I like to think I've been around; yet, in saying that, I have seen nothing quite so foul as heroin. In Harlem, I once walked around a corner and into a crowd of junkies, young kids, old men, hunkered down and shivering, half standing or sitting around a tenement stoop.

It was a scene of vomit and vacant eyes as I walked by, kids with bony arms pocked and scarred by needle marks, the old men in threadbare coats, unshaven and dirty. Later that evening, in a rehabilitation house, I watched the orgies of confession addicts must go through to clean out their minds and break the habit. Tales of whoring, crime and duplicity to get money to buy the dope. One kid wailed that at nineteen he'd seen more of his friends die than most people would at eighty.

Now heroin has come to Viet Nam. The Vietnamese are selling dollar-and-fifty-cent vials of crystal to GIs all over the country. The pushers are hooch maids, street boys, cyclo drivers, bartenders. Some soldiers prefer heroin now to marijuana. It has no odor and can be hidden easily. No fuss. You can mix the crystals with tobacco and light up in front of the MPs if you want.

The heroin, starting as opium grown in Burma, is so pure that mainlining is unnecessary. The crystals can be "salted" in cigarettes, taken like snuff ("snorked" or "snorted"), or stirred into a glass of beer at one of Saigon's new "skag bars." Many GIs believe they'll avoid addiction if they don't mainline. Which is partly true. Without the needle, they get only "candy" habits. This is a relatively mild tolerance; a real addiction, but it can be kicked with less pain.

Heroin is new to Viet Nam. Its prominence isn't widely known, and I've stumbled onto the story by luck. An air force colonel has been court-martialed for smoking marijuana with his troops, and though grass is Viet Nam's oldest story by now, the editors want a "situationer" pegged to the colonel's odd case.

Marijuana in fact, *is* a big deal. At least to the authorities. For there were 318 grass arrests in Viet Nam in 1966, and more than 8000 in 1970. I rarely meet a draftee in the field who doesn't smoke. But lately I'd missed the real news. All over Viet Nam GIs are using heroin.

An army officer assigned to deal with the problem tells me during an interview there were only 4 heroin-related arrests in 1966. In 1970 there were 1751. The army noticed the change last summer. Suddenly, huge shipments of nearly pure heroin began arriving in Saigon, Cantho, and Da Nang. The Chinese opium syndicates had seen the market: discontented and lonely GIs fresh from America's sixties drug culture.

I started talking around. A lieutenant I know says medics at a firebase he worked on near Phan Thiet were nearly all heroin or morphine addicts. He takes a variety of drugs himself and has friends who do. We arrange a photo session for the article—still on marijuana—in a barracks room near his office. We light candles and play music. Everyone smokes grass while a photographer moves around the room, bent over to get good angles.

Then I meet Spider, who frequents a "shooting gallery" named Mom's down an alley near Tan San Nhut air base. GIs gather there after work to get stoned in a variety of ways. Ron Ridenhour and I drop by one afternoon and scare everybody by just standing around, straight. One stoned black GI, coming down from heroin I think, pulls a knife and waves it around. He isn't looking directly at us, but we leave anyway.

Then I meet two navy men who no longer use it. They introduce me to a young "drug awareness" officer who is touring the world studying GI drug habits. He knows a lot of legal ways to get high, and he doesn't arrest people. The sailors seem to trust him. We walk around Saigon looking into skag bars, and he tells me a few stories.

The best tale comes out of the Laos invasion. Some infantrymen, he explains, keep heroin in the last bullet of their cartridge belts. A kid will unscrew the shell, empty the gunpowder, and pour in white crystal. Somewhere near the Laotian border last month a stoned machine gunner accidentally fired his "skag bullet" during an ambush. The bullet had no gunpowder, but its primer popped. The slug went into the chamber. The next shell was fired and collided with it. The gun blew up. The kid survived and everybody had a good laugh.

Heroin itself is no laughing matter. But then, neither is Viet Nam. Some GIs use it simply because sergeants are making it difficult to keep marijuana around—they need to get high to stay sane, and they don't care how. As I write this story, following it down alleys, into bars and in the painful faces of men I meet who use heroin, I am thinking of the costs of war. Who would have thought *this* would be one? A drug that destroys you while it helps you get away—for a while—from a war nobody sober would bother to fight.

Waiting to Go Home . . .

Walking on an air base near Cantho last summer, I suddenly became aware of a young soldier's eyes. I looked up to see his fingers, hard against his chest, form a "V" as if it were a secret. He moved them away from his body, then back. No one could see the "V" except me. I nodded and gave him one in return.

That was nothing new, of course. Young GIs here have always liked correspondents. Our stories sometimes make trouble for their officers, and we live and talk in ways that suggest the freedom they miss. It is easy for them to say hello or flash a "V" sign, offer C rations around a campfire—perhaps even some stash.

I saw more in this man's eyes: an alienation beyond traditional military discomfort. Almost a conspiracy, identified by the eyes, felt by men bound in common hatred.

Now, a half year later, the "V" seems trifling. Stories of murder and maiming are filtering down to Saigon: guerrilla war between hip, street-hardened draftees and the older careerists.

The careerists are dying—"fragged" in their hooches, mess halls, outhouses. Men are killed in fire fights now from AK-47 rounds where no Vietcong soldier was firing. It is so bad the army is counting fragmentation grenades. This accomplishes nothing, because Vietnamese civilians steal them from warehouses and sell them to the GIs on the black market.

Other explosives are available, and they are being used. A young lieutenant makes a battlefield mistake and the outhouse he is sitting in goes up in smoke. A hooch, home for two hated sergeants, explodes in the night. A major with a southern drawl finds the ignition of his truck wired with grenades. A sergeant loudly orders a hooch of black GIs to turn down the rock 'n' roll one night. He is blown into shards of flesh and bone two hours later when a grenade is tossed under his bunk.

The army is cannibalizing itself. There is no "mission" in the military sense. The president talks of bringing men home. Antiwar rhetoric is fashionable. Today's draftees are teen-agers and college students who watched America change its mind during the 1968 Tet offensive. Everybody wants out. Yet the firebases are still filled with young men risking death as if they were the rear guard for someone else's exit.

Now the young soldiers, like men in ghettos, have begun to mirror their environment. Despair and racial hatreds grow. Drug use increases. Violence erupts over meaningless incidents. Career military men, who misread the new mood, die. And Americans, once so pleased with this crusade, watch their children kill each other.

Street Scene

April 2

Midnight. Kids playing badminton in the glow of a street-light among deserted restaurant stalls. They knock the shuttlecock high into the darkness, laughing in tiny voices.

A rat eats out of a garbage trough by the curb and I stop to watch. The rats near my house usually run when you approach. But this one keeps on eating. Another gray shape, a smaller one, creeps out of the shadows, sees me and runs away.

The children gather round to see what's going on. The rat keeps eating. The smaller rat runs across the half-lit sidewalk and one little kid no taller than my armpit throws a rock which nearly hits its head.

The little girl behind me, maybe eight years old, jumps past me aiming a karate kick—barefoot—at the rat eating from the trough. It dodges and runs into the shadows.

She wears cheap black pants and a peasant blouse and now she picks up the racket and hits the shuttlecock again. They are still hitting it and laughing as I unlock the gate of my apartment and walk up the stairs in the dark.

Another Bar Girl

The girl in the Palace Bar tonight is long and slim, sharp and seductive, trying to con a drink out of me yet playing it as though she really cares whether I care about her or not.

I won't buy.

She stays anyway, telling me she doesn't want to be taken cheaply; and I listen, wishing it could be real, fantasizing in brief moments that she really is someone I care about.

She wants a drink.

I won't buy one, and I tell her that I like her but I don't want to be part of all this. I am trying to get rid of her nicely. But I am half serious when I say she is sharper than most, prettier, and I would like it to be something beyond this.

It won't be.

But I tell her that nevertheless I wish we could have a relationship beyond buying drinks. A friend turns around and says why don't you take her to dinner.

Impossible, I say. So he asks her on my behalf.

She says no, and we return to the routine about the drink. I say I'll get serious if she buys *me* a drink. Nice bluff.

She buys one.

No way to get out of this.

So OK, I say I'll buy a drink. She says she wants the more expensive version now—and that tears it. No deal, but she won't take the cheaper version, either.

I've been through this a hundred times. I am sick of placing money alongside of personal relations, I say pathetically, but please, please understand; I know you

155

have to make money. I don't dislike you for that. Just make it somewhere else.

She stays a few more minutes, sits beside me. Makes me feel bad and makes it seem . . . almost . . . as if there is something between us. Then some Americans, three of them, come in, and she excuses herself politely and goes over to them.

On American Values

Calley was convicted this week. I am assigned to talk to soldiers about him. About 45 minutes out of town, Delta Company of the Twenty-fifth Infantry Division has returned from the field. I am taken to their run-down enlisted men's club: The Hole in the Wall.

"Calley?" shouts one grunt above the noise, leaning over a pile of beer cans. "You mean the infamous Lieutenant Calley? He shoulda got a promotion!"

More than a dozen GIs laugh noisy agreement. The club is crowded and hot. A television is on, and between nude pinups and motorcycle pictures there is a poster saying, "Love is all you need."

"He's a hero," says another kid, after a long drag on his wet can of beer. "We've been in the same kind of situations—but our CO wouldn't let us do it."

More laughter around the table. The grunts are playing with me?

"Let me get this straight," I say, looking at the ring of faces. "You believe that Calley is getting screwed—that the war justified what he did?"

"There it is! Those guys were getting blown to hell. There *had* to be VC sympathizers in the area."

I glance at another wall poster: "War is unhealthy for children and other living things."

A voice cuts in.

"I don't think he got screwed," says a lean redheaded GI named Martin Esham, who walked up while they were talking and stands at the end of the table. "If the facts even approached what was reported, he deserves to be punished."

The table erupts in jeers.

"Get outta here," shouts one grunt. "You don't know nothin' . . ."

"Bullshit," says another just as loudly. "You never know when the gooks are VC. Kids carry grenades. Women know where the mines are. It's you or them."

But Esham holds, smiling the way you do when you are outnumbered, standing alone.

"Calley fucked up," he says firmly. "It doesn't matter if this is a war or not. He did something wrong and he's getting punished for it."

Something is happening. Everybody is thinking about this. There is almost no sound. Then one GI turns to look at Esham, then back to look at me.

He says slowly: "I hold with him."

More silence. I am thinking I would like to buy Martin Esham a beer, maybe a case of it. I owe him a lot. For without him, I would have had to write a story about human beings as killers.

"OK," says another. "I'm not gonna kill kids." He looks around the table. Then to please the other side he says, "But if I were in the same situation, I woulda at least killed all the men."

Nobody says anything for a while. Then a GI on a stool starts the conversation again. "Everybody shoulda been indicted," he says loudly, "or nobody."

"Roger that!" comes the chorus. "Up and down the line. From Westmoreland on down—or nobody!"

Then the kid who held with Marty Esham mumbles something to his beer can.

"It's the army, man," he says bitterly. "You pass the buck to the lowest man. You gotta get somebody, and Calley's the man they got."

It is quiet now, and everybody at the table seems to agree.

Antihero

"James, James!"

The voice behind my front door mixes anguish and enthusiasm, and it demands attention. The door is shaking. I pull it open.

"You OK, Ron?"

I am annoyed, and I'm joking to cover it up. Ron is an impatient, occasionally rude friend. He doesn't knock on doors and wait for them to be answered. He shakes them.

"Of course, James. Of course."

He fills the door with his arm-swinging football player's strut, walks to a chair and throws his bulk into it. He lights a cigarette and inhales deeply.

A newscaster on the radio says that America approves of First Lieutenant William Calley. Draft boards have resigned en masse, polls are overwhelmingly in his favor, politicians are speaking in his defense. Middle America fiercely supports the runty lieutenant convicted of murdering Vietnamese civilians.

Ron listens silently, smoking the cigarette and letting his head fall back over the top of the chair. He blows a huge cloud of smoke toward the ceiling. Nixon has let Calley out of jail for the court appeals, saying he'll "personally" review the case. It seems that the country has risen to say no American should be punished for killing Asians.

And Ron Ridenhour, the tough ex-GI who first reported My Lai to Congress and the Pentagon, feels as though all America hates him.

"Fuck 'em," he growls, slumped in the chair. "They deserve me."

Ron is big—about two hundred pounds of bone and

muscle, big arms, broad shoulders—and hard in a mythical American way. Sometimes I call him "buffalo hunter," after a steely character we saw one night in a John Wayne movie. He likes this. He is from Arizona, a lonely man hailing from a metaphysical frontier of America nearly forgotten—an odd mixture of individualist, man and boy. He can be thoughtful, bright and creative, and he can be a petulant kid, stubborn and hotheaded and unable to take advice.

He came to Viet Nam the first time as a draftee, and his refusal to bow to the pettiness of army authority made him a constant headache to authorities. After serving as a helicopter door gunner—and telling a sergeant off in excessively plain language one day—he became a "ranger" team leader for reconnaissance patrols. It was a dangerous assignment, and he did it well.

In both jobs he killed Asians. Yet he fought by the rules of war, and in and out of combat, he has an outraged sense of right and wrong—a laserlike vision which cuts through complexities and often forces him to cause trouble.

That's why he reported My Lai.

Tonight Ron is in pain. A radio commentator, a minority voice, is analyzing American reaction to the trial as we listen now—and condemning it. Ron rises out of his chair suddenly and stretches his arms toward the radio as if it were a lost brother. His face is a mix of powerful emotions festooned by triangular sideburns that travel along prominent cheekbones and merge, Gay Nineties style, with a wide moustache. His hair flops down over his forehead, resting above angry eyes that offer no compromise, ever.

We turn it off and go out to dinner. On the way to the restaurant, we pass groups of soldiers. I feel them staring. They probably don't recognize Ron, but I *feel* their eyes, somehow resentful. Ron, head high, is a ship pushing through heavy waves. I'm following in my rowboat.

"I guess I'd better write her," Ron says morosely about

a girl he knows in the United States, "and tell her she's not hooked up with a popular man."

I nod. The statement doesn't seem at all corny tonight.

We have drinks at the restaurant bar, then dinner, then back to my place to talk before I turn in. He lived in a spare room at my house for nearly five months. Then I moved to another place and he found a small apartment in another part of town.

He talks in a drifting, almost casual way: the first time he was told about My Lai, his shock, how he checked unit records for the proof. Then from others he heard the story again and again. He began looking for people who could tell him about it. It is odd. I've known Ron all this time and have rarely asked him about My Lai. Ron doesn't want to be a hero—he's never taken a dime, he says, for his trouble, despite offers of television and lecturing. He remembers going home, arguing with parents and friends about what he should do.

Nearly everybody said to forget the whole thing.

We have been friends since he returned to Viet Nam last August for a year of free-lance reporting—a difficult role to play in Saigon. You have to live off leftovers, the jobs that staff people don't want or can't get to. Money is scarce. And while Ron is willing to work, he can't escape his reputation. He is young, just beginning a hoped-for writing career.

But tonight and tomorrow the strain of his past is great—the strain of forcing his country into a test of principle. And tonight, in the realization that America doesn't support him, Ron feels very alone.

Good-bye

We had a strange thing going. She was slender, blonde and blue eyed, hair falling in ringlets and curls around a warm, flushed face. Her eyes—glassy eyes looking through you—signaled serious conflict inside: a pink-cheeked American girl trapped in a private nightmare. She lived in Milwaukee a long time ago. And once she tried to kill herself there, stumbling as blood began to trickle from her slashed wrists and passing out before she cut herself deep enough to die.

We met last fall in Katmandu. I was on vacation, lost in the mysticism of mountains and temples. She appeared on the second day, looking up at me, almost as in a dream. She smiled and talked of the mountains, where she had been traveling for a month, and I fell suddenly in love with her. Later she talked of her life. The escape from her family to a communal farm in Wisconsin, then to New York's East Village; and finally to Wales, in backpack and blue jeans, to work with retarded children on a country estate.

Then, inexplicably, she left. Another year passed as she pushed slowly across Europe and the Middle East, resting finally in India. By now, she was dropping acid and shooting heroin and one day hepatitis arrived on a filthy syringe. Half alive, she crossed the mountains to Nepal, there to rest and perhaps find peace. Soon afterward, in a mirror, she saw an old woman. And she gave up heroin. She grew stronger. The day we met, she took a friend's coughing baby to the hospital at midnight—saving its life, doctors said.

I asked her to come to Viet Nam to be with me. She said yes. Somehow, in a crazy way, I thought it would work. I left Katmandu the next day, and she hitchhiked

162

shortly afterward to New Delhi to fly to Saigon. And while I waited, and she traveled, something changed. The translucent eyes had turned gray, barely flickering when she arrived. And as she looked around to see jeeps and fighter planes, they lost their light altogether. For a while she seemed happy when we were alone. But Saigon and the war destroyed whatever we had. At night she would start to ask questions, then stop—unable to express what she felt.

I needed her—or something I thought she was. But it couldn't work, and she knew it first, and finally we stopped pretending. I didn't see her for a while after that, and then one morning she came to say the government was kicking her out. She was a drifter, some money from a trust fund to keep her going; no goals in life that the Vietnamese government could understand.

She'd begun working with orphans: the deformed, unloved and living refuse of Saigon. No one was paying her—she wouldn't take money—and she wanted to stay. One night, earlier, one of them died, a kid reaching stringy, half-dead arms out to her from his bed. For days after that she wouldn't talk about children or anything else.

She came for help. Could I talk to someone, get her visa extended? At first I didn't want to help. It meant seeing her again and confronting the pain I felt. But I arranged some connections at the American embassy that, in the end, didn't work. That was three weeks ago.

And tonight a bomb exploded at a nightclub we used to go to. She was there. We both loved the club, the lights and its rock band called the CBC. Everything there was up: good music, warmth, the colors, the crowds of GIs, noisy happy nights we spent there.

And tonight someone blew it up. She was sitting in the back row, alone. A thousand firecrackers. And the ceiling started falling in, she said.

Some GIs pulled her out, and dazed and dusty she ran into some friends of mine on Tu Do Street. They called me and I came down from the office and we sat on the hotel terrace. She was frozen with shock and held my hand hard, as if without it she might fall off a ledge. Then she softened and finally talked about leaving. The government deadline was Monday.

After an hour, I broke away, leaving her with the friends, and went down to the wreckage. The bodies were gone, but the building looked as though lightning had struck. I took some notes for an article; then, walking in the rubble, I found a bottle of champagne which had survived the blast and took it back. You got blown up, so have some champagne. And she laughed a little and said she hoped everything would be good for me after she left.

I wanted to protect myself. For a moment, it was pure Bogart. I smiled a little. My voice became hard. OK, you have a good life, too. She smiled again.

Suddenly she stood up and started kissing me in front of everyone. And they kept talking and we held each other and I felt I was splitting into separate parts. I had to leave, to sit alone and listen to some music and try not to think what I once felt about her.

A Little Love

Lights low. Strobes blinking, Day-glo posters on the
walls. GIs drumming on the tables, laughing and drinking beer. The kid on the drums rocks the rafters with a
pile-driving beat, the girl's voice is rich purple, the lead
guitarist arranges as if he's been in the business for years.
Hendrix, Beatles, Led Zeppelin, Credence Clearwater—
a *happy* place.

It is twenty-four hours after the explosion, and I am
sitting at a typewriter trying to write about the CBC.
Those are the initials of a Vietnamese phrase meaning
"two brothers and a sister," and the group plays better
music than I can remember hearing anywhere except
New York or San Francisco.

And they combine cultures beautifully. Vietnamese
and American values usually mix disastrously in this
country. But on the CBC, chains of peace symbols and
long hair over burnished skin and almond eyes look
right—so fine that I would drop in night after night (the
band would wave when I came in with the girl from
Katmandu) for injections of their heavy music. Raspy-
voiced Loan, the sixteen-year-old lead singer, did Janice
Joplin as if they had identical tonsils. Vann, the drummer,
who is fourteen, was christened "the little master" by
the foreign correspondents.

For more than a year before I discovered them, they
were a favorite among young GIs. Their reputation
grew and the Young Sound Nightclub was filled to capacity most nights—a khaki Café Au Go-Go.

And a perfect target for terrorists.

The band was rolling into Jimi Hendrix's "Purple
Haze" last night when the building came *apart*. There

was a huge crunch and the sound of things breaking. Boards and plaster flew around. The ceiling fell in, and dust and debris and smoke filled the darkness. "Suddenly it was very loud and the lights went out," Loan told me today. "Everybody was yelling and screaming. I couldn't see at first—I thought my eyes had died."

Terrorists* had left forty-four pounds of plastique against the club's street-side wall. When the timing mechanism connected, the bomb blew the wall and the ceiling down. A black GI died in surgery after he was pulled out of the ruins. A Vietnamese girl died instantly when a board shot through her chest. Thirty-six people were hurt. The club was blown down and the kids were out of business. All of their sound equipment was destroyed.

I visited their house today, a small bungalow down a long alley too narrow to drive. The kids had only cuts or scratches, but it was a depressing time. Both the music and the money are gone. They truly loved the music—practicing even on days off. And the money supported an extended family presided over by a betel-chewing widowed mama-san in a conical hat and black pants. She took them home in a pickup truck after each night's performance.

For the most part, Saigon bands are creaky imitations of the early Beatles. But CBC, which includes two cousins on backup guitars and a tiny girl with big eyes named Marie (also a cousin) who sings second to Loan, had gone beyond that. The kids were professionals in a way that belonged to no single culture. And they were proudly antiwar, a new generation of children for Viet Nam, exchanging "dap" handshakes with GIs, sometimes smoking joints with them.

Most important to me, they had a *feeling* to share: some joy in unhappy, violent Saigon. Something I fool-

---

* Terrorists, maybe. A friend who worked for American intelligence came through New York as this book went to press. He'd looked into the incident and is convinced a rival nightclub owner set off the bomb.

ishly thought safe until last night. Now CBC is crippled and the gloom has shaken everyone I know.

I took pictures at the house, and then Linh, the lead guitarist with shoulder-length hair who sometimes struggles with his English, leaned over to say something.

"We play good music and we say peace," he started.

He paused, groping for words while the others nodded. I noticed a bloody scratch on his sister's face as she watched him.

"But someone didn't want to make peace last night," Linh concluded unhappily. "Someone wanted war."

Cambodia: The Last Time

I'd forgotten its beauty—the lines of trees along shady avenues, gold tips of Sihanouk's palaces above them, a tranquil river barely ruffled by boats. The night, as before, is still. I walk through it, and memories fall into place easily. I'm back for a few days to do a political story. Lon Nol has resigned, probably temporarily, and all is turmoil among the bureaucrats and politicians below him.

My mind searches the city for changes. More traffic: generated by thousands of refugees who've fled the countryside in the last year. The streets seem narrower, the buildings more crowded. There are more uniforms, and there is more barbed wire. More military trucks on Monivong Avenue. Signs of a culture being changed.

Little things. Dance halls open in the afternoon now and close at 8:00 P.M., though it is still the same twist and jitterbug music, "The Tennessee Waltz," and the dark, pouty girls in long Khmer dresses. Near the river I knock on the locked door of a favorite bar. No answer. Others open up, but again, you have to knock first. Legally they should be closed.

At the Miami Bar I talk to a girl who once worked for Air Cambodia. She speaks several languages and had flown regularly to Hong Kong, Singapore and Djakarta. Now Air Combodia runs rarely and she is out of work. Her husband had joined the army. He was killed. She has two children. She has a round, pretty face—and gets depressed, choking a little, when I ask questions. She drinks too much, and she is gaining weight. And she knows it. She'll sleep with me if I want. The offer comes with a sad, sensual smile. She is pathetic and sexy in the noisy half light of the bar.

I'm supposed to find out why Lon Nol resigned. He had heart trouble a while ago. After a seizure, the American embassy sent him to a heart specialist in Hawaii. He returned still paralyzed in the left arm and leg. He has difficulty speaking. He came back to an airport which is broken, like he is, and barely functioning. The Vietcong blew it up in a spectacular night raid, destroying most of Cambodia's air force in the process. The main building is half in ruins and looks like an unfinished public works project, construction materials and workmen scattered about. Most business is transacted in a downtown office.

Thousands of Cambodians waited for him as the government plane touched ground. When he stepped out, he was barely able to clasp his hands in the traditional greeting, fingers skyward, touching, head bowed. Since then, it has gotten worse. He is said to be emotional—withdrawn, angry—about the paralysis. His closest advisers are feuding. Cabinet factions trade charges of corruption, and many Cambodians have begun to realize the war will continue for a long, long time. And for now, it goes poorly.

I spend the week talking to all sides of this. I am bent over a typewriter one night trying to make sense of it all. A few more days to follow leads, then out again through the battered airport to return to Saigon. It is hot again and the river is quiet and the children fly kites in the parks which surround the gold tile spires of the empty royal palace. It pulls together into a last memory of this troubled place, a pocket of fragile beauty in my mind on the brink of being lost.

The Great Brass Caper

May 15

It begins in a bar. Ron is sitting on a stool, waiting, when I arrive at midnight. He hands me a notebook. No words, and his face is hard. He'd said on the phone that it couldn't wait.

The note I am reading says there is a classified army report, recently sent "eyes only" to the White House, telling how high-level Vietnamese generals and politicians are indirectly selling American-supplied brass shell casings to Mainland China. The traffic involves millions of dollars. I let out a deep breath and look at Ron; he nods, smiling cynically.

The brass arrives here as live ammunition. It is worth about a thousand dollars a ton, and by treaty agreement it cannot be sold. Despite this, there is a thriving business in exported brass. It is taken off battlefields, stolen from munitions dumps, sometimes stripped from live shells. Then it is smuggled, often in Vietnamese army convoys, to ports up and down the coast.

There it is flattened, put into barrels and loaded by night into freighters bound for Hong Kong or Singapore, where it is bought by middlemen who regularly sell metals to China. Follow this further. China supplies nearly a third of North Viet Nam's military aid, including ammunition. So the shells thudding into a northern region firebase last night, or the bullet killing Infantryman Joe Smith today, may have come, in part, from America.

That is, with an assist from Saigon's generals. They are selling our bullets to the other side. My eyes widen to half dollars, reading this. I've been in Viet Nam nearly fourteen months. I'm tired of war and ready to go home, and I've seen a lot of corruption. But compared to this, everything else was small change.

We go to the office to wire a few details of the story to the editors in New York. The cable is marked "confidential." This means all copies should be taken off the Saigon machine and returned to me in a sealed envelope, avoiding the "out" book which anyone can read. I write the message at 2:00 A.M. and go home before the operator finishes.

Next morning the cable's carbon copy is gone. There is nothing to do. At least three Vietnamese in the office work for the army or the police.

We fan out to separate sources—intelligence, army, political—and it soon is obvious we have a major story. I tell a Vietnamese cabinet official about the report and he looks a long time at his hands before answering. "No matter what we do," he says softly, still looking at them, "we cannot win."

Now he stares at the wall. "We have been afraid for months this would come out. But *why*—with antiwar demonstrations, the mood in the American Congress, smuggling, heroin problems—why *now!*" Then he regains an Asian mask, and tells me very little.

An American embassy source admits to Ron, yes, he knows about the case. But that's all he'll say. President Nixon is personally reviewing it, and Ambassador Bunker and General Abrams were briefed six times in the last two weeks.

Later he tells someone else: "We're sure the stuff is getting out of here in large amounts, but we can't prove it."

And he pauses.

"One reason it's so hard to prove is that investigation is extremely dangerous. When so many people are making so much money, they won't stand by and let someone find out about it—or report it. It's easier to kill him when he gets too close."

We keep going. An finds a Vietnamese source who promises to produce a palace copy of the report. But this takes time, and when it arrives we get nothing but the part that defends the Vietnamese government. Pieces of the story however, begin falling into place. We are told that commanders of three of the four military regions have been smuggling brass for years. A woman at the airport controls much of this and other illicit traffic such as drugs and black-market money. Ask about one kind of corruption, it seems, and you get multiple answers. There is an under-the-table buying and selling operation in black-market goods, we are told, in the presidential palace, though not in brass. Next comes word that one ARVN commander operates—ready?—a heroin factory. A CIA source admits the factory exists, though he won't confirm that the general runs it.

The entire bureau is working on the story now. Stan Cloud, who works in Bangkok, flies in. Donn Downing, who has arrived from Los Angeles to take my place, gets involved. One night Stan, Ron and I meet in a restaurant. Ron and I feel uneasy about the story. We've been told one army investigator's life was threatened. Another was shot at. Ron and I are beginning to see shadows and guns everywhere—looking behind as we talk as though someone is listening. Stan scoffs at this, but as we tell him more about the story he too feels the fear.

We decide to ask Ron's original source, an army major who sees intelligence and investigative documents, to a private dinner. Army officers rarely talk openly with us. But this one is unhappy with military life and upset over the corruption he sees around him. He approached Ron through an assistant, a lieutenant who sent a note to Ron's table in a Saigon restaurant.

When they met, they talked mostly about heroin traffic, but in passing—almost as if it were an afterthought—the major mentioned the other report. Ron asked if he could get it. No, but the major remembered parts of it and described them. That night Ron called me.

The major is blond, and he looks like an Ivy Leaguer in khaki, wearing wire-rimmed glasses. The lieutenant comes to dinner too. During the drinks before dinner, the lieutenant toys with a camera he says he just bought, as if fascinated by a new plaything. Then he snaps pictures of all of us.

The dinner yields no new information. The major talks about himself, shows us unclassified papers, and asks what we've found out about the case. He leaves and we are in disarray.

Is he investigating *us*? If so, why bait the trap with such a hot story? Is he after Ron—who has been shadowed by army investigators several times since returning to Viet Nam? I argue the major is straight, if a bit strange, for he's brought us a story that will embarrass people whom his superiors would rather protect.

But it is hard to dismiss the fear we all feel. And five minutes after he left, the major returns. He says he forgot his glasses. Was he listening behind the door?

The next day we call an American official who is said to be reviewing the case. He agrees, with visible nervousness, to see us. I don't go but the others say he seemed frightened when they arrived. He asks what *we* know. And when the others admit we have only outlines, he clams up.

Back to point zero.

I see a friend who speaks fluent Vietnamese. He has been in Viet Nam five years and deals in intelligence. He knows about the case but only dimly, he says. It is out of his "area." We'll never document it, he offers helpfully, for nothing is committed to paper in Viet Nam. And when Vietnamese talk to Westerners about corruption, they never talk publicly. He adds, smiling: "There's probably a brass export requirement for every gun in the country. The Vietnamese are very quota minded." Commanders, indeed, may be firing twice as many shells as needed to get the casings.

He goes on to explain the tradition of corruption in Asia—and how it has ballooned out of normal proportions here. Most landlords, for example, take rent only in dollars now. The deal is private and they beat the tax man by sending the money to a Swiss bank. Respected generals and politicians all over Viet Nam bring heroin in for American GIs. They also traffic in opium and black-market goods. Everyone knows this, no one can prove it. A rubber-plantation owner north of Saigon pays taxes to the Vietcong. How else could he survive? And many of Viet Nam's generals, we now find, sell brass indirectly to North Viet Nam.

We have a story, but pieces are missing. We can't get a copy of the army report, though we know it exists. We have a lot of related fragments. The American fired for helping a Vietnamese subcabinet official ship the brass out. Quotes from a score of sources describing parts of the operation. Stories of Vietnamese officers who are involved. The story of a Vietnamese convoy carrying brass coming out of the American Ninth Division's just-closed base in the Delta. Dozens of names.

So we expand to a "corruption in Viet Nam" piece—throwing in heroin problems, gold transactions and corruption at the ports ("I've seen some ship captains on the verge of tears," an American source tells Ron. "There's not a goddamn thing they can do about it, and they know it.").

This is, of course, an admission of failure. We are close, but not close enough to do the story by itself, laying out the full case in detail. I am angry, but then I would have been surprised if we'd gotten it. For after fourteen months, this country remains a parade of shifting shapes and shadowy light in my mind, its truths essentially hidden. The questions of death and power and greed are never resolved. Each story seems important when you do it—or *try* to do it—but the stories are only shrubbery on an expanse of earth that you rarely dig into. Viet Nam will not be changed by the presence of reporters. Or even armies and bombs. The good and bad of it endures, and will not change.

And this story, its complexity, shadows, danger and glimpses of evil, sums up much of Viet Nam for me. The printed result of our efforts will be a muffled look at corruption that holds no one specifically accountable. The story is a metaphor for the war. Historically, no one seems accountable for Viet Nam, either. Lyndon Johnson loses the presidency. William Calley goes to jail, maybe. But as monuments to history, each is too small a man to blame for a decade of war and hundreds of thousands of lost or ruined lives. Viet Nam endures. The Americans, poorer for having been here, move on.

That is all.

One more try. The weekend before I will leave Viet Nam forever, a friend reports seeing a truck piled high with old shell casings headed for the harbor. I run for the car. Photographer Dave Burnett is along and we speed blindly toward the water. And there, lumbering along the crowded river road, is an old truck with so many rusty shell casings in it that, like the pieces of our story, they seem poised to spill in a hundred fragments about the street.

We give chase. Dave leans out of the car snapping pictures furiously. I pull up behind, close, then back, so he can get the angles he needs. The truck crosses a bridge with cyclos and motor scooters in a clogged, smoky traffic pattern. We are excited as hell. It turns into a wharf area and drives past an armed Vietnamese guard. We stop, thinking this is the end, but he lets us pass.

The truck moves down a long dirt road, ships to one side, warehouses opposite. The mud and gravel are studded with fallen casings. At the road's end, I think I see the end of the story—thousands of shells stacked in an uneven mountain in front of an old Chinese freighter. A dozen men and women, sun dried and skinny in conical hats, load them into large rope nets. These are hoisted over the side and dumped with a clatter into the ship's hold. I am thinking we've finally done it.

Looking nervously around like characters in a silent movie, Dave and I take more pictures and toss a couple of shells into the back seat. The ship sits at the far end of the road. It would be easy to be caught here, I am

175

thinking, surrounded and taken apart. But Dave and I speed out without incident. In our Chaplinesque frenzy, we think we've made a great coup.

We haven't.

We find out the casings are mostly iron with brass primers, the result of a *legal* scrap sale to an American businessman. Iron isn't worth much. And the brass in them has been declared. ("We don't trust the guy," an Embassy source admits, "but he's legal.") So the pictures are wasted. I had planned to lead the story with a description of the brass piled high. That is gone. Nothing remains except to laugh at myself.

Why, then, do I bother to tell this story? A story of failure and fuzzy conclusions? Because it says much about my time here. About Viet Nam. And the American experience in Viet Nam. The half truths and failed humanity. And the pain that follows every story—how much it matters for a moment in time. And how little, you finally realize, it *really* matters. How, when my time comes next week, I will get on a plane and sail out of Viet Nam, a leaf lost in a gale wind, riding out alive with feeling and yet scarcely noticed as I go.

For there will be a bullet tomorrow, or next month after I am gone, that kills a man with friends and family. They will grieve for him; and elsewhere, someone will lift a glass of Cognac paid for by pieces of brass brought to Viet Nam to wage a foolish war over a democracy that doesn't exist. It all came together briefly in a story that a small group of reporters tried to put together.

Going Home May 22, 1971

Two bulging suitcases. Camera bag. Briefcase. Type-writer. The guitar—I never learned to play it—is packed in a Pan Am shipping crate. So are paintings, jade sculpture, stone rubbings, silver jars from Cambodia. And the war leavings: Vietcong money (one VC note pictures people shooting down American helicopters where, on a dollar bill, George Washington would be), a scrap of metal from a burned-out Russian tank at Lang Vei, the mortar tail I picked up at Thanh My, my fatigues and jungle boots.

The gray business suit I came in is packed away. I'm wearing dungarees, feeling tanned and sinewy, tough-ened by the drama of the year, relieved to be alive and unhurt—as if I'm exhaling after holding my breath for a long time—but still lonely behind wire-rimmed sun-glasses and a little frightened about the future. I'm taking the long way home, stops in Nairobi, Cairo, Vienna, Paris, finally New York. Maybe I'll shave off my beard in Paris. I don't know.

Chi Ba is waiting at the door. She's crying and I hug her for a moment, strangely moved by this. I think I was good to her—but tears? Somehow I don't expect her—or any Vietnamese—to cry at my departure. So thank you, Chi Ba. Tears come easily in this country—I remember unhappy children in refugee camps and a young prosti-tute crying in Cu Chi—but they are valued no less. Le Minh is waiting outside with a car and I toss the baggage in the trunk.

It is nearly lunchtime. I spent the morning writing a few last lines on the brass story. Jon Larsen, whom I shall miss a lot, grinned over my shoulder while I typed, en-joying his mock Simon Legree role. The last days slipped by quickly in the heat of the brass story. And there were dinners to attend, gifts to buy, trunks to pack, airline tickets and visas to get. Add drinks at the corner café with friends. Piaf and Elvis Presley on the scratchy jukebox again. I was afraid each time would be the last.

I've been thinking about this day for months. Time in Viet Nam becomes a terrible burden. For a while after arriving the country is fresh, the war dramatic. Then night falls and you want—desperately—to get out, to leave this confusion of death and dying things. As a journalist you are powerless to stop the dying. Sometimes one story will have a small effect, and more stories will have a bigger one. But mostly you can only hope the dying misses you, write about it, regret it and leave.

And so my time is gone. A particular Thursday I've long thought about is here. It is time for a strange dislocation, pieces of me left behind in a proud culture, friendships formed that can't be equaled in New York, my mind reaching out for things to hold onto as the time slips away. Glad to go. Sad to be leaving.

Jon rides out to the airport with me. We have bowls of spicy Vietnamese soup at the café. He talks of stories to come and people he has to work with, and I am touched by the emotions I see in his eyes. Pain? Friendship? They seem to show I will be missed. I am listening to Jon and thinking too, of people I will miss. And the rawness of last year, growing older in a hard, difficult way—but suddenly my mind turns to Bangkok and Bombay, the first stops en route to Africa and Paris. And home. And now a last handshake, walking to the plane and looking back, carrying my typewriter and briefcase and lifting them in a last wave to Jon and Le Minh and the war and the heat and the part of me left forever behind.

This book has been set on the linotype in Caledonia
The display type is Melior
The composition is by
American Book–Stratford Press, Inc., New York
The paper is Sebago Antique
The printing and binding is by
H. Wolff Book Manufacturing Co., New York
Designed by Jacqueline Schuman